LADDER

TO THE

LIGHT

"Here is wisdom born out of a lifetime of listening faithfully to the voice of God. Here is wisdom we need for the living of these days."

—Rev. Michael B. Curry, presiding bishop of the Episcopal Church and author of *The Power of Love*

"This book touched me as few do, which I take as proof that the author is in cahoots with the Spirit. Steven Charleston is a spiritual medic who has given himself to a life of healing, and you will want to share his medicine with everyone you know."

—Barbara Brown Taylor, author of *Learning to Walk in the Dark* and other books

"What an anchoring book—the wisdom in it is distilled through many traditions, and is available to us all!"

—Bill McKibben, environmental activist and author of *Falter* and other books

"*Ladder to the Light* isn't a book to be read once and put aside, but one that should be read again and again, becoming part of our human journey. I highly recommend this book for all who are searching for a better way of belonging."

—Kaitlin B. Curtice, author of *Native* and *Glory Happening*

"Defying conventional notions of religion, Steven Charleston places our feet on a trail of faith, blessing, and hope, leading us to truth and transformation. Through Native traditions and culture, we see a new vision of today's society—a tribal community of human beings moving toward justice as we search for the sacred."

—Thom White Wolf Fassett (Seneca), author of
Giving Our Hearts Away: Native American Survival

"Steven Charleston's book is a prophetic guide to the life of faith. He masterfully weaves together the wisdom of Indigenous theology with the voice of the Spirit. Charleston illuminates the way the Spirit brings us into its loving presence, transforming us into a people equipped to do the work of love for ourselves, our communities, and our world."

—Sarah Bessey, author of *Miracles and Other Reasonable Things* and other books

LADDER

TO THE

LIGHT

AN INDIGENOUS ELDER'S
MEDITATIONS ON
HOPE AND COURAGE

STEVEN CHARLESTON

 Broadleaf Books

Minneapolis

Note: The author is a citizen of the Choctaw Nation. Connect with him on Facebook @bishopstevencharleston.

LADDER TO THE LIGHT
An Indigenous Elder's Meditations on Hope and Courage

Cover design and illustration by Faceout Studios

Print ISBN: 978-1-5064-6573-9
eBook ISBN: 978-1-5064-6574-6

For Choc and Billie

CONTENTS

INTRODUCTION

THE VISION OF THE KIVA

If you have ever traveled among the Native American nations of the Southwest, you are probably familiar with the kiva. The kiva is a square or circular underground chamber, covered by a roof of wooden beams with an opening in the center. You enter a kiva the same way you enter a submarine: by descending the ladder. Once inside the packed earth chamber of the kiva, you are in darkness. Without a fire in the kiva, the only light comes from above you. To reach it, you have to ascend the ladder.

The kiva is sacred space. It serves the same function as a cathedral, as a place of worship. Yet while a cathedral's soaring arches or a mosque's great domes are designed to point us upward, the kiva is intended to point us downward. The spiritual focal point is not above us, but below. We are not to look up, but down. What we seek is not in the sky, but in the earth.

This dramatic shift in our spiritual orientation is important. The kiva points us in a new direction: not an escape from this world, but an entering into it. The kiva is a womb. It is a place of origins. It is where, according to my ancestors' teachings, life first began. As the tribe of the human beings, we began our existence in the womb of the earth, beneath the surface, in a place of darkness. Through many different incarnations of life on this planet, we finally emerged into the light. We climbed the ladder not to heaven, but to home. We came out exactly where we were supposed to be: in this reality, surrounded by all the other life forms of creation. We emerged ready to begin our migrations across the globe, discovering more light wherever we go.

The spiritual resilience of North America's indigenous peoples is legendary. Our traditional religious practices were banned. Our sacred objects were taken from us and either destroyed or put in museums as a curiosity for our conquerors. Our families were scattered into diaspora. Even our languages were forbidden.

But we are still here. Our voice is still strong. Our vision is unimpaired. Native America knows something about resisting darkness. It is what we have been doing for more than five hundred years.

The kiva symbolizes this spiritual resilience. It reminds us that we began in darkness—not the stark, ominous darkness we imagine we face today, but the nurturing darkness of the womb, a place of formation and growth. Over time, through the grace of the Spirit, we learned more, understood more, until we matured and were ready to take our place in the bright world of reality. We emerged from Mother Earth. At first we were weak and unsteady on our feet, like any newborn. But with the support of the earth's other creatures, we soon stood up together, formed communities, and began living in the way the Spirit instructed us.

My purpose here is to lift up the kiva as a metaphor for our contemporary spiritual situation. In that context, the vision of the kiva is not just for Native Americans, but for all who will receive it. It is a symbol for our shared future. It tells us that if we are in a time of darkness, we need not be afraid of it, because it is only the beginning for us. In other words: we have been down this spiritual road before. The kiva tells us we have been through this process of birth and rebirth more than once. As a people, we have entered into darkness before, only to emerge into light.

To help us understand the kiva's contemporary relevance to our situation today, let me share one encounter that illustrates the kind of darkness I believe we inhabit. Several years ago, I was standing in a parish hall at a church in New England, speaking to an audience of largely professional people with comfortable incomes. They were well educated, well read, and alert to the news of the day. By all of society's measuring sticks, they should have been among the best and brightest and most optimistic, the bedrock of an enlightened spiritual community. They should have been confident, but they were not. In fact, they were just the opposite. They were worried.

The depth and nature of their worry was revealed in how they responded when I asked them to name one institution—one public system in our culture—in which they still had complete confidence.

Would that be in our educational system? I asked. The room was silent.

Our political system? Silence.

Our judicial system? Silence.

Our health care system? Silence.

How about our religious institutions? Surely we still have confidence there? More silence.

As we looked at each other in the silence, we understood something profound: we are a generation that no longer believes things work. We no longer take it for granted that any of the social systems on which we depend to sustain a healthy community can continue to do so. In this darkness, we are beset by questions that make us uncertain. Can we live together in peace when we disagree? Can we accept the idea that change and tradition are not mutually exclusive? Can we realize that diversity is an innate human characteristic? Can we understand that our ecosystem is a survival pod with limited range and resources? Can we learn that having more for the few is not as important as having enough for the many? The questions become a world of shadows and fears.

I do not believe the people in the New England parish are alone in their doubts. Any reasonable look at American culture today would verify a pervasive unease about the path our society is taking. It does not matter whether we label ourselves conservative or progressive; the reality we share means many of us are losing confidence. We are worried. The ground seems to be shifting beneath our feet. We no longer rely on the institutions we once felt were our firm foundation. We are afraid, and we are looking for a way out of the darkness and into light.

This book is a ladder into that light. Each rung of the ladder, each chapter of this book, is a spiritual vision. Altogether, there are eight rungs to climb, starting with the first step in our spiritual understanding and ending with the final rung that takes us to freedom.

The substance of these visions began long ago, far from New England, far from the kiva, out in the open-sky country of rural Oklahoma, where I was born into an extended Native American family. As a four-year-old, I would sit with my great-grandfather beneath the star-filled sky as he told me stories from my ancestors and stories from the Bible. When I asked why he was telling me these stories, he said, "Because one day you are going to be *pehlichi shilombish* [a spirit guide], and you need to know how things really work so you can help others find their way."

Maybe it was that upbringing in Native American tradition, or maybe it is just my own nature as a spiritual seeker, but for more than seventy years, I have tried to be open to the Spirit's messages. I have been a listener. I have been a collector of visions. I have been a guide along the spirit paths my ancestors first discovered so long ago. Then, about

a decade ago, I began receiving the sacred story in a different way, one I could neither have imagined nor predicted
when I was a little boy. I discovered this path by accident.
It began in an unlikely exchange between my ancient traditions and one of the most common technologies of our current reality: social media.

Some people who knew me wanted me to join them on
Facebook, but I did not want to be on social media. They
persisted, saying I needed to catch up to the rest of the
world in technology. Finally, I relented, but after I had been
cajoled into it, I had no idea what to post. By nature, I am
an introvert. I am not good at making small talk. And if you
are familiar with Facebook, you will understand when I say
I have no pictures of cats to share. Once I had created my
account, I stared at the blank screen, wondering what to
write. I did not think my life was all that interesting, so I
decided to simply write down whatever came into my mind
each morning after my prayers.

Day after day, morning after morning, I say my prayers—
outside, if weather permits—in a traditional Native American way. I start by acknowledging the four sacred directions
that encompass my life in the holy geometry of creation,
then I acknowledge the earth beneath me and the sky above
me, and finally I speak to the Spirit in humility and remain
silent to hear what reply comes into my heart.

It is these replies—these brief messages from the
Spirit—that I decided to share on Facebook. For over ten
years, I have been posting them. At first, only a handful of

people noticed. Now, thousands of people read them daily. This still amazes me. I would never have thought of connecting Native American tradition to Facebook, but it has happened, because while I am the writer of these words, I am not necessarily their author. I believe a spirit inspires what I write—not because the language is so eloquent or the meaning so profound, but because the words seem to help people from many walks of life. Perhaps they will help you too. Perhaps that is why you have picked up this book.

This book is a collection of the Spirit's messages, arranged in sequence like a ladder, one rung after another. I began writing this simply by following a year's worth of messages I had shared on Facebook, as if they were rungs on a ladder. I imagined I was in the kiva, in the place of spiritual beginnings, then I started climbing up the Spirit's messages to see where they led. The result is a series of sacred messages linked together to form a ladder we can use in finding our way out of darkness and into light.

Chapter 1 is the rung of faith. The ascent to light begins within each of us. It is our ability to trust what we cannot see. Chapter 2 invites us to step onto the rung of blessing. The strength to climb is a gift we receive. It is the acceptance of grace as a reality, not a wish. Chapter 3 is the rung of hope. The more we climb out of darkness, the more we see the light to come. It is the dream unique to every human soul. Chapter 4, then, shows us the rung of community. As we climb, we recognize that we are not alone; community sustains us. The climb we make is not easy, so chapter 5 calls us to step onto the rung of action. It changes the shape of reality and confronts the powers that seek to keep us in darkness. Chapter 6 is the rung of truth. The integrity of the climb we make is measured by the nature of the light we seek. It is the honesty of the journey, not the destination, that matters. Chapter 7 is the rung of renewal. As we near the end of our climb, we realize we have been changed. We see clearly because we are looking through the eyes of hope. Chapter 8, the rung of transformation, means our climb is ending. It is ending in the emergence from darkness into light. It is what we all create together when we give more than we take.

As I climbed the rungs of these messages, I paused to write my own commentary about them. If you are a movie fan, this may be easy to understand. Many films offer a version in which the director comments on the movie as you watch it. What you will find in these pages is similar— you will be reading the messages I received from the Spirit woven together with my interpretations of them. You will see the Spirit's words of inspiration—the writings I describe as messages—in italics, and my own reflections and interpretations in regular print.

Taken together, the Spirit's messages and my commentary are the ladder. Just as you might do when you climb any ladder, feel free to take breaks on your ascent. Pause on any given rung to catch your breath or to meditate before taking the next step. If a particular message seems to capture your imagination, stop reading and take the time to dwell within that message. That might take an hour, or it might take a day. Time is not as important as meaning. Take what I share here and make it your own. The kiva and the ladder are the sacred metaphors I use to describe a spiritual process that can take any person of any faith tradition from the darkness of worry to the light of hope. The vision of the kiva is not for me alone, but for every person who picks up this book and begins their own climb to understanding. If I have learned anything over the last decade of sharing messages with listeners, it is that the messages I share and the images they create are capable of being translated into an infinite number of personal journeys and faith traditions.

Consequently, when I speak of the Spirit in this book—which I will do a lot—I need to be clear about to whom I am referring. When I transcribe what I call messages from the Spirit, I use broad language for the sacred. I did this unconsciously at the start, but I have continued to do it because I want as many people as possible to feel at home in my writing.

I use the word Spirit as a marker—a placeholder—for the conscious, spiritual presence many people from different religious traditions would call God, or the creator. Full disclosure: I believe most people of faith are not one-dimensional beings. Instead, we are made up of many different spiritual practices and a lifetime of experience. We are the sum of many parts. For example, I am a Christian. Many years ago, I was ordained as an Episcopal priest on the Standing Rock Sioux Reservation. I have served as the Episcopal bishop of Alaska, I have been a professor in various academic institutions, and I have fulfilled administrative roles for seminaries and for the Episcopal Church. I am also a follower of my Native American tradition. I am an elder in the Choctaw Nation of Oklahoma, and I believe in my ancestors' faith as embodied in many different tribal traditions and ceremonies. Finally, I am a practitioner of Zen meditation; I honor the teachings of the Buddha. For me, the Spirit has many meanings that arise from this ground of faith.

The Spirit I refer to can represent the Holy Spirit of Christians, the Great Spirit of traditional Native American wisdom, or the Buddha-nature in all living beings. For some, the Spirit may signify the underlying force that binds all life together, like the Tao. It can be understood as God or Allah by Jews and Muslims. It can embody Brahman for Hindus. It can be the collective human spirit for humanists.

I intentionally leave the interpretation open because my messages are not dogmatic—that is, they do not demand conformity to any one system of belief. Theological debates are for another day. My messages are spiritual invitations to any person who can find themselves in the words I share. In this book, I want to throw the doors open as wide as I can to welcome people from every walk of life. This ladder, these messages, are meant for all of us: the human family, the tribe of the human beings. So although I may write about the Spirit from my own spiritual context—for example, I come from a matrilineal culture, so I refer to the Spirit as "she"—I want every reader to feel free to interpret the nature and meaning of the Spirit for themselves.

Why? Because a crisis of confidence is occurring around the world. The challenges we confront are global, therefore the only effective response we make will have to be just as universal. We cannot squander our energies on fighting the usual historic battles about our various doctrines and creeds. That is an argument for a different time and a different place.

My role in writing this book is what my great-grandfather first predicted: I am only a guide pointing the way to the ladder. My task is articulated by the first message I chose from my yearlong collection of prayer responses from the Spirit. When I first began praying about writing this book, I turned to this message:

AN OFFERING OF PEACE. *I have achieved few things in my life worth noting, but one thing I have achieved is important—not because of what it reflects about me, but because of what it may offer to you. I am a person at peace, at peace within myself, at peace with the world around me. All my other faults are intact and fully apparent, but deep in my spirit's core, I am a calm soul. What does that mean? According to the ancient tradition, it means I have something I can share. The peace I feel is not something I am to keep, but give away. So, please receive the one true thing of value I can give: this offering of peace for your life.*

These are words about me, from me, but they were written down under what I believe was an inspiration from the Spirit. They are simple words, honest words, and words that open the mind and heart to deeper insights and emotions. Whenever you see italicized paragraphs in these pages, know you are reading one of the messages I transcribed over a year of prayer.

Today, people around the world read and share these messages. I do not believe that is by accident. It certainly is not because of any planning or design on my part. I think I backed into doing this for a purpose. The Spirit is trying to tell us something. She is trying to get us to think and act together.

Why? Because we are going to need one another more than ever in the days to come. If the light seems to be failing, the darkness cannot be far away. A second message spoke to me as I began building a spirit ladder in the kiva:

STRONGER THAN DARKNESS. Imagine you walked onto a large open field at night when there was no moon. Standing there silently in the darkness were hundreds of people, each holding an unlit candle. Only you were carrying a candle that was burning, a single light alone. How quickly would the field be glowing once you used your candle to light others, and they used their candles to do the same, and all the people began sharing their light with those around them? You may never know exactly, but you do know over time what the outcome will be: a field aglow in the darkness where people can see one another clearly. Your life matters. What you have started will carry on. You are a source of light. You help others in ways that will continue. You are a single candle, but you are stronger than darkness.

The metaphor I use to name what is troubling us in this generation, what is threatening us as a global community, is a term just as broad and generic as my use of the word Spirit. It is darkness.

The classic conflict between light and dark speaks to people of all spiritual traditions. It is the fear of what we cannot see and cannot control: the dark forces of power that come against us, the bleak future we dread but cannot seem to avoid. Darkness is what the New England parish saw all around them when they were sitting in silence. They were in the kiva and did not even know it. Darkness is what you and I can see as we look at the daily news. We are in the kiva right now.

This book, this ladder, is for all of us who have been standing together in the darkness. It will call us to be a new light for one another, to form community, to work together, to share in a common love that transforms reality and promotes justice. It will call us to see ourselves as the tribe of the human beings, a community still in the kiva, waiting to be born.

We have all been to the dark places, the shadowland just next door to what we call reality. There, clarity is lost and doubt dwells. There, we are uncertain about what tomorrow will bring, if tomorrow can come at all. The dark places can appear slowly or suddenly, but either way they cover us in a fog of doubt, leaving us feeling alone. It is at this moment that faith becomes our compass, for it reminds us that darkness is only a detour, never a destination. These small corners are not the true landscape of our lives. They cannot contain the power of love. Then the Spirit calls for us until we find our way, out of the dead end of worry and back to the broad and bright streets of hope.

We inhabit a period in history that seems to be filled with conflict. The world has become an uncertain place, a dark place, where we cannot see what may happen next. All we know, based on our recent experience, is that things could—and probably will—get worse. We are losing confidence that our institutions can prevent this. We are losing confidence in our leaders, because they seem to only make it worse. We may even be losing confidence in ourselves to help things change. It is no wonder that we are anxious. We feel the earth beneath our feet is unstable. We see darkness all around us.

But you are stronger than darkness. *We* are stronger than darkness. That is the vision of the kiva. That is the ladder to light.

And it is a powerful vision because it arises from a wisdom more ancient than time itself. For millennia, my ancestors followed a spiritual path that was respectful of the earth, inclusive of all humanity, and visionary in its transformative power. That tradition has survived. It is one of the oldest continuous spiritual paths on earth. My ancestors' faith continues to this day despite every hardship and persecution it has been forced to endure. Not long ago, I was asked to write a brief commentary about the Christian theology of the apocalypse: the final, terrible vision of the end of the world. I said my Native American culture was in a unique position to speak of this kind of vision, because we were among the few cultures that have already experienced it. In historic memory, we have seen our reality come crashing down as invaders destroyed our homeland. We have lived through genocide, concentration camps, religious persecution, and every human rights abuse imaginable. Yet we are still here. No darkness—not even the end of the world as we knew it—had the power to overcome us. So our message is powerful not because it is only for us, but because it speaks to and for every human heart that longs for light over darkness.

We are all in the kiva together. Whatever our politics, whatever our religion, whatever our culture, we are all in the darkness together. We can see that as a frightening place to be and begin fighting among ourselves. We can be afraid and scramble for the ladder, pulling one another down in the process. Or we can take this moment as a period of deep spiritual formation. We can renew our faith in the Spirit and in one another. And then we can climb. We can begin our ascent from darkness together, in the confidence of our faith and in the commitment to the light we strive to share.

This book acknowledges the darkness. It understands the fear. It speaks a quiet confidence to anyone who will hear a word of hope. It reminds us that we are each called by the Spirit to be a source of light for others. It shows us how we gather strength in our diverse community. It gives us the power of hope. It invites us to make an exchange of our wisdom. It tells us what we can do to help.

It gives us the promise of the light to come—but more importantly, it shows us the way to reach that light.

CHAPTER I

THE RUNG OF FAITH

> *MADE FOR FREEDOM. We are not made for resignation. Passive acceptance is not the code written into our spirit. If that were true, as a species, we would have vanished long ago. Instead, for millennia, we have shaken off the temptation to simply accept reality and the demand that we bend the knee, and we have stood up to struggle against the odds, to change the situation, and to find an answer and a healing. Those deep drives are the energy we call hope. Those active forces are what determine our future. We are not made for resignation, but for freedom.*

Many people today are living underground. They are living in darkness because they cannot clearly see how history is unfolding. On the surface, things seem chaotic. Culture wars continue to rage, dividing people into opposing factions. Political parties become entrenched. Governments become gridlocked. Social institutions appear ineffective in restoring confidence. The courts are jammed; the prisons are overflowing. Racism creeps into any open space it can find, and old fears of human sexuality crawl into the fractures that separate us. Religion preaches a good game, but it seems unable to sway the hearts of humanity toward hope. Law is less about keeping order than keeping control. The gap between those living in luxury and those struggling to make ends meet grows wider each day.

Meanwhile, the greed that drives exploitation ravages the earth, stealing any inheritance of beauty from our children and giving them a future with more natural disasters, pandemics, and conflicts than we have ever known. Right now, a small number of people absorb an enormous amount of what the earth can give. She cannot give more, and when it is all taken, there will be none left, not even for the few. The light toward which we climb is the light of common sense. We recognize that we will have to make some deep changes. We will need to find sustainability. We will need to establish balance in the use of resources, in the fairness of distribution, and in the ethic of justice for all. Peace is not free; it comes at the price of entitlement and privilege. Before we put a single foot on the ladder, we must be prepared for what it will take to reach the top.

Is it any wonder that many of us feel our only option is to keep our heads down? We go underground. Emotionally, psychologically, and spiritually, we go underground. Some of us confuse the kiva with a bomb shelter. Believing the world to be irredeemable, believing the worst is yet to come, we take the survivalist option to find a private hideout and stay there. In our cynicism, we think every man is for himself. We decide to grow used to living in darkness, accepting our reality as a fearful place we cannot change.

For my ancestors, however, the kiva was nothing like a bomb shelter. It was a waiting room. A place of new beginnings, formation, wisdom, and transformation—the kiva was underground not as a shelter, but as a seed. Its darkness was fertile, not fearful. The image of the kiva was the image of a womb, an environment redolent with the power of creation. In this spiritual context, going into the kiva was going underground for a positive reason: to be closer to the generative forces of the Spirit.

Is the darkness above a reality? Yes, it is. Is the darkness in the kiva real? Yes. I see the darkness all around me, just as you may see it and just as the people in the New England parish saw it. But I see darkness in the kiva the way my ancestors did: through the eyes of faith.

Faith is the first rung on the ladder to light because faith is perception. A long time ago, my ancestors came to view the world with a profound spiritual understanding: we do not believe because we see; we see because we believe.

SACRED JOURNEY. There are no shortcuts on the spiritual path, although many have tried to find one. Learning the lessons the Spirit teaches takes time, patience, and perseverance. It requires a sense of discipline. It takes a level of self-awareness that can be difficult, because it requires that we are honest with ourselves. We have to look deeper. We have to study. We have to live a rule of life that never takes love for granted. It is not easy, but it is joyful. The sacred journey may take us up some very steep hills and demand we keep going even when we are tired, but it also shows us the wonder of life along the way and the purpose of life when the day is done.

Faith is perception. It is how we see. If we see the world around us as nothing but darkness—a darkness we believe we cannot change—then darkness is what we get. But if we see darkness while we believe in light—a light we cannot yet see but know is there—then we get something new: we get possibility—the possibility of change. It all comes down to trust.

The first step up the kiva ladder is the step of trust. Do we trust our own vision? Do we trust in love? Do we trust in a truth greater than ourselves? The answers that we give to these questions are the rung of faith. While we are in the kiva, in the darkness, we begin developing our spiritual vision. Even if we cannot yet see the light, we imagine it. We believe in what is not visible, trusting that our own spiritual instincts, our own sense of love and justice, will reveal to us a light that can change our reality.

> STUBBORN OF SPIRIT. I don't know if I am spiritual or stubborn or a combination of both. But the more the bad news piles up, the more determined I am to respond to it with the good news I feel so clearly in my mind and heart. Yes, life is hard. It is full of suffering and sorrow— and believe me, I have had my fair share. But life is also beautiful, full of moments that are transcendent in their healing and love. I know because I have been blessed by more of them than I can count. I cannot change the reality of pain or loss, but I can claim the reality of grace and joy. Maybe I am just stubborn, but I want my last word to be not a complaint, but an alleluia.

We gain this level of determination through our trust in the Spirit. In fact, our degree of commitment can often be measured by our degree of faith. The more we believe there is a force for good working alongside us, the more we are willing to keep going. We recognize our source of strength. We believe in a power that can do what we cannot do by ourselves.

BURN BRIGHT. The flame of life burns brighter when touched by the breath of the Spirit. The more we are open to the presence of the sacred in our lives, the more we find energy to do those things we only now imagine. Inspiration is not just an idea, but a movement, a tipping point toward creativity. It is what we believe opens our hearts and minds to discover new ways to share our lives with others. Spirituality is an exchange. Through it we receive the strength of the Spirit so that we may give our love more deeply. Burn bright in faith today, for with the Spirit all things are possible.

Faith—that is, seeing by believing—gives us the ability to do far more than we ever imagined. We often sell ourselves short. We think we are not great leaders, that we have no special gifts, that we are too small to make much of an impact against such serious obstacles. But the more we trust in the Spirit, the more we trust in ourselves. Faith gives us both the energy and the ability we need to believe in the possibility of change. It teaches us that we can make a difference.

SPIRITUAL ADRENALINE. In moments of crisis, the adrenaline in our bodies can give us extraordinary strength, allowing us to do things we otherwise would never be able to do. The same is true for our spiritual adrenaline, that strength of faith within us that kicks in when we need it most. It is the power of the Spirit channeled through us by grace. It helps us to face challenges of illness, grief, and stress. It keeps us going when others grow weary. It lifts our vision to see the way forward. Faith is not just a refuge, but a source of resilience. It lets us move mountains and face down giants. It is the great release of pure spiritual energy we call love.

While we are empowered to do more than we imagined, we are not called to do more than we can. A great deal of our activism in the Spirit is accomplished in simple ways. We are not asked to be heroic. Most often, it is enough that we remain consistent in living out our faith in small ways.

THE SMALL THINGS. In the end, it may be the little things that make the difference. While we were distracted by the major issues of life—the big-ticket items of careers and relationships, the things we accomplished, the hurts we endured—it may be the small things that slipped by unnoticed that changed another life for the better. We do not need to be in the spotlight to bring light into another person's world. We do not need to be onstage to play our part in the drama of life and love. We need to be only who we are, as loving and kind as we can, for blessings to flow through us into another heart, unknown but forever grateful.

We do not need a spotlight to bring light into our lives. When you are in darkness, even a small candle can seem like a great light. We develop our trust, our faith, one small action at a time. We can do that in a million small ways every day. It happens in the choices we make, in the way we translate what we believe into how we behave. We develop our skills at generating light not only for others, but within ourselves. Faith is not something given; it is something grown.

> DISAPPOINTMENT. One of the spiritual skills we need to practice is how to deal with disappointment. Prayer is not a vending machine. We sometimes do not get what we request. Life can constantly surprise us, and not always in a good way. Someone else gets the job we wanted. Our bright idea is passed over by the very program we helped create. It is not easy to come in last. Disappointment is the price of admission for trying, and it often teaches us more than success. Wisdom is the value of trying again, and it offers us more than we first wanted or ever expected.

When we internalize our trust in the Spirit, we grow stronger in dealing with disappointment. We turn from focusing on what we cannot do to what we can do. It is often said, for example, that my ancestors practiced their faith on a daily basis, but what does that actually mean? How did they do that?

Here are three examples from the messages I received from the Spirit, three small steps we can take on the rung of faith: create memories, give generously, and find time to laugh along the way.

1. CREATE MEMORIES

DESIGNERS OF MEMORY. One of our most important spiritual jobs is to make memories. Our task is to help those for whom we care to increase the number of memories they have that make them smile, make them feel appreciated, make them know they are loved. We do this in many ways, some complex, some simple, but all made with our unique touch. We are the designers of memory. We are the architects of experiences that last, moments so happy or so kind that they are transformed into the longest-lasting possession any human being can have: a memory. Memories may be with a person until the day they die. In the end, the memories we make are our most enduring achievement.

2. GIVE GENEROUSLY

Another spiritual practice that creates light is generosity. Generosity is an ancient practice, one that has been recognized as integral to spiritual life for thousands of years. It is not a question of how much we give, but how often and why.

MORE TO GIVE. The more you give, the more you seem to have. That's one of the beautiful discoveries of the spiritual life. It is a wisdom you gain more by doing than by thinking. Like most spiritual knowledge, it is counter-intuitive. You would think if you give something away, over time you would run out, but that's not how it works. The more love you give away, the more love seems to grow within you. The more compassion you share, the more compassion you have for people and animals. Offer one act of kindness, and suddenly you can do ten times as many. Abundance in days of scarcity: the more you give, the more you have to give.

3. LAUGH ALONG THE WAY

Even our sense of humor is a spiritual gift we can use to intentionally reshape the reality around us. Laughter is stronger than darkness.

FULL OF WHIMSY. A little laughter along the way never hurts. A few smiles, sprinkled like brown sugar on oatmeal, help keep our daily reality from becoming relentlessly static. Life is hard enough. We need our sense of humor like a lifeline, bringing us back to balance, keeping things in perspective, offering us a chance to see the light even in the midst of darkness. The platypus and the camel are with us for a reason. They remind us that at the core of creation is a heart full of whimsy. Laughter is a gift with a purpose, for when we laugh, we pray. Death may frown, but the soul finds a reason to smile every time.

It all begins with the first rung on the ladder to light: our internal decision not to be passive in the face of darkness, but to be active through trust in what we believe. Seeing reality through faith shows us there is always something we can do each day that will make a difference.

WORK TO BE DONE. Every day I know there is something I can do to help, something great or small: showing up, being counted, attending the meeting, making my contribution, saying my prayers. Something I can do to make a difference, great or small: volunteering, offering to drive, passing on the information, telling my elected leaders how I feel. Something I can do to spread the word, great or small: make some ripples, open hearts and minds, change the world for the better. Every day I know there is work to be done for the good of others, for the good of my planet, for the good of my soul. Every day is a good day to do something to help.

Trust is essential to faith because in the darkness we cannot always see our way forward. We can stop climbing when we are uncertain. Faith is not about what is absolute and unchanging, but rather what is uncertain and ever changing. Faith and doubt are eternal dance partners. The spiritual life does not demand that we be unquestioning in what we believe. Just the opposite—it requires us to question everything we see in order to find a faith in which we can believe.

CROSSROADS QUESTIONS. What next? Those two little words ask one of the biggest questions in life. Where do I go now? What do I do? These are crossroads questions, the ones we all have asked ourselves when we have been searching for a direction in life. Choosing a direction is making a decision. Making a decision is an act of faith. Even if we think we have no faith at all, we do when we take the next step on a path we have decided to make our own. We believe in our choice. We hope it is the right one. "What next?" is a prayer, whether we realize it or not. "What next?" is an invitation for the Spirit, who stands at every crossroads to offer a word of wisdom, if only we will listen.

In the spiritual life, we all have a job description to fulfill. In two of the messages I received, this is seen in the image of a spiritual medic or a spiritual construction worker. These are different images, but they carry similar messages: We are here for a reason. Our lives are entrusted to us for a purpose. It is not always an easy or glamorous job, but it is the vital work of restoration, reconciliation, and renewal that must be done, and done on the run in the face of rapid changes.

SPIRITUAL MEDICS. I think you and I have been recruited as spiritual medics. We may not have asked for the job, but under the current circumstances we have been pressed into service. It is a tough world out there. Socially, economically, and politically, people are struggling around us. People are anxious, angry, and afraid. They are divided and uncertain. Conflicts are increasing. Into this reality the spiritual medic is called upon, again and again, to risk being a target in order to bring a healing word, to risk the safety of familiar trenches to stand on open ground for the sake of peace. We won't win any medals, but a lot of people are going to be glad we were there when they needed a little help believing in tomorrow.

Another image that underlines the important nature of the work we are called to do is that of a building site. By our own choices, we are building the world our children will inherit. We are making something every day, for better or for worse. Our spirituality is not just soft sentiments and wishful thinking, but hard outcomes generated by the daily decisions we make.

SWEAT EQUITY. I guess you could say I have a working-class spirituality. I think you have to put a little sweat equity into what you believe. You have to practice what you preach. Justice does not just happen. Compassion is not a spectator sport, but something I have to exercise as I roll up my sleeves to do my part in creating a better community. I need to put in my hours as a volunteer. I have to join the prayer crew and put my life on the line to make a difference. The world will change not by wishes, but by the labor of love we call faith. Spirituality is not a spa, but a construction site, where we build hope one heart at a time.

Whether as a medic or as a construction worker, we need to remember we are here to serve others. This is not all about us and it never has been. It is about community. It is about the tribe of the human beings. We have a constituency as people of faith. There are other human beings and other life forms we work for.

AN OCEAN OF LISTENING. They are listening. The poor are listening for the word of justice to give them hope. The lonely are listening for the sound of a caring heart. The abused and broken are listening for the healing sound of mercy. The fearful are listening for a word of truth that can set them free. Many people listening, but what are they hearing? Break their silence with the sound of the words the Spirit has given you. Speak hope and mercy, speak justice and truth, say what you believe that will heal and help. Now is not the time to be quiet, for there is an ocean of listening all around you, waiting for the word of life.

If they are listening, what are we saying? This first rung on the ladder is where we give our answer. It is where we claim what we believe. We may still be in darkness, but we have one small light to follow. We know there is something greater than ourselves at work in the world, and we know we are part of it. We have a purpose. We can make a difference. When we begin to believe that about ourselves, we begin to see things more clearly. The darkness begins to recede.

What made my ancestors strong, what allowed them to survive, was faith. A faith practiced every day, recreating reality one step at a time.

SPEAK OUT. Speak out the hope you feel, for the world around you is longing to hear it. Speak out the story of mercy and forgiveness, of justice and respect, of the simple decency of the human heart when it reaches out to help another, for many around you have lost sight of these things in the dim light of a troubled age. Speak out on behalf of those who have no voice—the creatures of this earth—for they are dependent on wisdom alone to save them from the rush to profit. Speak out, for silence is what kills the dream. You have a clear vision, a strong faith, a loving spirit—speak out and heal what is broken.

We live in the dim light of a troubled age—that is, the darkness we confront and that we seek to transform. Through the practice of our spiritual lives, we can accomplish an alchemy of hope. We can transform the base materials of our own experiences, the hard parts of simply being human in a difficult time, into something wonderful and enduring for our community.

THE GROUND OF LOVE. My sorrows are like seeds, pressed deep into the dark earth of my soul. I do not deny them. I do not forget them. But nor do I let them remain unchanged. Over time, I let their pain turn into wisdom, their grief into mercy, their anger into forgiveness. Hidden within me, I let the hurt they once carried become the compassion I now carry, compassion for all who have known what I have known, felt what I have felt, wept as I have wept. The ground of love transforms the seeds of sorrow to new life, new hope, new beginnings, through the mystery of soul-deep healing. I do not leave my faith fallow, but I use my brokenness like a garden until it turns loss to gain and tears to songs of joy.

Spiritual practice is daily practice. Each day we make the choice to believe, to be hopeful, to do our part. We turn what we believe into what we see. Therefore, we see possibilities, the little fireflies of hope that fill the kiva with the promise of the light to come. With faith and through faith, we work for justice, for the poor, and for the creatures without a voice of their own. Simply, we stand up.

THANK YOU. Thank you for standing up when many others are sitting down. Thank you for speaking out when many others are silent. Thank you for walking forward when many others are stepping back. These are not easy days, but days of choice and challenge, when every person hears clearly the call of conscience and must decide to act or wait, to watch or do, to give or withhold. We walk on edges, not along wide paths. We take chances, without rewards or recognition. These are not easy days, but days that will be remembered. Thank you for being part of it now, when it matters the most. Thank you for being here now, when history is still being written and hope is new in the hearts of those who gather.

Once, not long ago, I was invited to attend an international gathering of women in Brazil. I was honored to be one of few men invited. When it was my chance to speak, I looked out at hundreds of women from every part of the world—from Africa to Asia, from the Amazon to the

Himalayas, from Palestine to Michigan, women from many different communities but with a shared experience of darkness. I cannot remember everything I said, except that I shared a simple message of faith. I asked them to stand with me if they believed we could overcome that darkness. One by one, they stood up. All of them—hundreds of women who had faith—stood together, unafraid and confident. That is a sacred memory I will always carry with me: the power of faith standing up to darkness.

DON'T LOOK. Don't look down, don't look back, don't look away. Don't look down with your head bent by sorrow or fear, for the courage you have within you is reason enough to hold your head high. Yes, you carry a heavy burden, but you know you never carry it alone. Look up, for love still has much to show you. Don't look back to the old hurts and struggles, for they have had their moment and cannot live in the light of this new day. Look ahead to what life offers you now. Don't look away from the challenges before you, no matter how hard they may seem. Breathe in the strength of the Spirit and trust what guides you. Look your truth straight in the eye and capture the vision that will set you free.

Here is a mantra for our activism: Don't look down, don't look back, don't look away. Look up and be confident.

Look forward and learn from the past. Look at life as it is, without editing it to look better. See what is really there.

We each count in this struggle against darkness. We each have a role to play, and it all begins in the kiva, where we recognize darkness but trust in light. We take our first step on the rung of faith. We believe in what we cannot see but know is there. We take the time in the kiva to develop our perception, our skills, and our determination. We learn what it means to walk in faith.

WRITE YOUR NAME. *We write our names on the sky each time we do an act of kindness. We say "I am here" to the universe, imprinting our time among the glittering lights of creation, in the small spaces between lives. There exist the joyous markers of our passing, our moments of love and loss, our quiet hours of thought and deep reflection. "I am here," we announce to the heavens. Whatever happens, we have left our names on the hearts of those with whom we have shared the sun. Our memories echo down the valley of time, still heard long after we have made the journey home.*

You and I have a contract with the Spirit. We have a working relationship. Our purpose in creation is not just to sit and look pretty, but to stand and go to work. Life is unfinished. Hope is not yet realized. There is much to be done, and much of it can only be done by you and I.

FREE EXCHANGE. Each day the exchange is made: the Spirit offers me another day, and in return asks only that I make the most of it. The gift of life, of being with those I love, of seeing the sky and feeling the wind, of thinking and creating and being—all of this is freely exchanged for the promise within my soul, the possibility of great thoughts and caring actions, the ability to love, and the capability of change, if only I make the effort to meet the Spirit halfway. Each day I am grateful for the gift and more than willing to give what I have in return. If time is my measure, then let me fill it to the brim, pouring out my best, sharing my heart, loving all I can, giving all I have. Let no day be wasted, no chance taken for granted, no moment passed by unseen for the blessing it reveals.

You are needed. You are important. Your choices make a difference. Your decisions count. These are the elements of spiritual self-confidence we need to own for ourselves. They give us something to live up to, to aspire to, to recognize as an integral part of ourselves. It is our witness, our testimony, shared not by words alone, but by our actions.

The tasks we are given are never impossible, only difficult. Nothing we are called on to do is beyond our ability. We received that strength long ago, in the beginning, when we first made our soul contract with the Spirit, our bond of kinship, and our commitment to community.

LOVE AS STRENGTH. Let your love be your strength. You do not need anger or judgment, for they are mirrors of the soul that say more about you than others. You do not need righteousness or correctness, for these pretenses are always transparent. You do not need superiority or power, for they will always betray you to false pride. When you feel called to stand for what you believe, take up love as your witness. Love will shine through with the clear message you wish to convey. It will withstand any pressure to compromise your truth or bend to deny that truth. Love will unite your friends in struggle and speak to the hardest heart with whom you contend. Let love be your strength and you can stand before lions and never fear.

CHAPTER 2

THE RUNG OF BLESSING

WITHIN YOU. No words I write will be as eloquent as the *silence within your soul. At best, my language is only a key to unlock what is already written in your heart: the strength you seek, the answers to your questions, the healing for which you hope. It all is there, in the still space where you encounter the Spirit, the common ground between the holy and the everyday. It is a place where only you can go, where your own thoughts and words transcribe the truth of your experience, and where the voice of the Spirit can speak in whispers like the wind moving through the trees. No one can give you what you already have: the love of the Spirit within you.*

I am not a guru, saint, or prophet. I am not even an especially wise or good person. I am just another human being facing darkness, like you. I do not believe I have any special knowledge of that darkness, nor any quick fix to restore our world to balance. I do, however, have one card up my sleeve: I believe in the Spirit.

I believe in a power greater than any of us can truly comprehend. My ancestors called the Spirit Hashtali: the Vastness Beyond the Sun. That is exactly what the Spirit is—a vast consciousness present in creation at all times and in all places, and equally present in our lives, helping each of us do things that would otherwise be impossible. I have seen that happen many times in the lives of others, and I have seen it in my own life. I understand, therefore, that the second rung on the ladder to light is not one I take by myself. Alone, I might remain in darkness, but with the strength and support of the Spirit, I can continue my climb to the light. I rise through grace, not through my own power. I step out on what my ancestors called the Blessingway, a spiritual vision of life that is grounded in the healing ceremonies of the Diné (Navajo) people. It speaks to our need to walk in harmony and balance with all of creation.

When this Spirit touches us, it is called transformation, so the place to begin is within ourselves. Before we talk about darkness and how to overcome it, we need to talk about ourselves, about each one of us and our connection to the Spirit, because that is where and how the transformation begins. We turn from darkness toward the light when we are changed by an intimacy that is difficult to describe.

When people begin to follow my messages on Facebook, they often say, "Sometimes it feels like you are speaking directly to me." To this I reply, "Well, that's because I am." More accurately, if you believe in a higher power, it is the Spirit who is speaking to you. The words have an impact. They cause a response. They touch the heart and stir the mind.

This is not me. I do not know the inner thoughts and feelings of others. I do not have the gift of second sight, and I am as confused about reality as the next person. No, this feeling—this sense that someone knows you and is speaking directly to you—comes from the Spirit. She knows you, and when she speaks to you, you can feel it.

Accepting that reality takes a little processing. We commonly think the Spirit talks directly to only a chosen few, but I believe the Spirit speaks to all of us and the Spirit's message is critical for us to hear.

THE HOLY HAND. Do not doubt yourself, especially if you were programmed to do so by the critique of others, who told you over time you were not smart enough, not good enough, not pretty enough, not strong enough to measure up to their expectations. In childhood, in relationships, in sports, in schools, in marriages, and in old age—there are many fields in life in which the seeds of doubt can be sown. Do not harvest weeds, but claim the wisdom, the beauty, and the skill that are yours—the unique qualities that make you who you are. Do not doubt yourself, for the holy hand that shaped your soul is a maker of art. You are a masterpiece of mind and spirit, of endless possibility, of visions unseen by any eye but your own.

Are you a masterpiece of mind and spirit, a keeper of visions unseen by any eye but your own? I would be shy to make a claim like that, and I suspect you would be too. But there it is: the Spirit is speaking directly to you, to me, to any of us who want to follow a spiritual path. If we want to be light in the world, we have to believe we are capable of being that light. In other words, we have to believe in ourselves, no matter how much we have been programmed or conditioned not to by voices that denigrate us or make us feel inadequate.

In the eyes of the Spirit, we are not weak or small. We are masterpieces of endless possibility. The first step is accepting that possibility. The Spirit has faith in us; now we must have faith in ourselves.

LETTING GO. Let go of the worries that tangle your mind. Let go of the fear of the future you cannot clearly see. Let go of the memories that melt beneath your feet like quicksand, drawing you deeper into the dark waters of regret. Let go of every care that would steal your heart. Drop them all from your hands. Let them fall to the ground. They can hold you no longer. This is a moment you have given yourself, a moment let loose from all constraints.

By your faith you are free, alive in the liberty of hope. You have stepped into the circle of the Spirit, a space without the gravity of sorrow, a space open with restoration and renewal. Let go now and be healed.

Faith is a conscious decision. To embrace it, we have to let go of our fear. Faith takes effort. It requires us to have a new mindset about who we are and what we can do. Faith is not an idea, but an action. We let go of what we have been told to believe about ourselves. We listen to a different voice, one that comes to us from deep within our own soul. That is the voice of love. It is the Spirit telling us we are worthy and that we can overcome our problems, even if those problems seem as overwhelming as darkness.

COME OUT AND BE HEARD. Come out with me, out beyond the usual bounds of your life, out to the wilder places where you may rarely venture, out to see the limits of what you can do. You are the creator of a thousand ideas, the maker of imagination, and the designer of dreams. In a word, you are a thinker—still are and always have been. We need your kind of thinking now, that open-ended, imaginative, hopeful kind of thinking. We need your insights and your concerns. Come out with me, out into the wide world that has grown so weary—come out and be heard. Come change us with what you have discovered, with what you know, with what you think.

The messages I write often have a level of direct intimacy. On my own, I would not write words like these, perhaps because I lack the level of self-confidence the Spirit has. I do not think of myself as the creator of a thousand ideas, the maker of imagination, or the designer of dreams. That language seems inflated to me. But the Spirit will not let me get away so easily. She challenges me with what she says: *Come out with me. Work with me. Create with me.* She tells me what she tells you: *We need you. We need what only you have. We want to hear what you have discovered, what you know, what you think.*

In the messages I transcribe, I hear this kind of intimate affirmation over and over. It does seem that the Spirit knows me better than I know myself, and if I listen to her long enough, I realize she is right. There is more love, more strength, and more hope within me than I imagined. I have been so focused on darkness that I have failed to see the light within.

I SEE YOU HERE. "I believe in you," says the Spirit. "I believe you are a person open to new ideas, willing to listen to a different opinion. You are a critical thinker who can weigh the evidence for themselves. Consequently, you are a bit of a risk-taker. You are not afraid to stand outside the crowd, to be different from the rest, to be a free spirit. And yet you are not a loner, for your heart pulls you to care for others, especially those in the greatest need. In reaching out to them you make no distinctions, but show your kindness without condition. I know this because I see you here, among the friends of faith. And so, like them, I believe in you."

Over time, I have come to understand that so many of the messages talk directly to people about their value and self-worth because we all need that level of encouragement for the task we face together. As we will see in later chapters, a great challenge is before us. To meet that challenge, we each need to be confident in our faith.

THE ETERNAL NOW. Do not be afraid of change, for the eternal now in which you live, the changeless love that surrounds you, will take you through whatever is to come, bringing you safely to the embrace of the one who watches over you. You do not need to try to control every moment, predict every outcome, and struggle with every new reality. You need only to trust what your heart tells you: You are loved unconditionally, you are cared for unceasingly, and you are secure in arms that will never let you go. Life is within you, always. Change will come and go, but what you feel when you close your eyes in prayer will outlast even the stars above you.

This message of reassurance and confidence appears repeatedly in the messages I receive after my morning prayers. It is the substance of the blessing that is the second rung on the ladder, because it is an intimate expression of the Spirit's Blessingway. Just as the kiva is a vision of many of the Native American communities in the Southwest—specifically the Hopi and the Pueblo people—the path of blessing is sacred to the Diné, the people known to many as the Navajo. In their wisdom, the Diné understood spiritual transformation as the energy that allows us to climb from darkness to light. As the Spirit touches us, we are changed. We are healed, strengthened, and enlightened. Through blessing, we are enabled to face any challenge in partnership with the Spirit.

DO NOT BE AFRAID. Do not be anxious today, no matter how difficult your life may seem, for there is a loving presence watching over you. No matter where you are, no matter who you are, no matter what your circumstance, no matter how serious your situation, there is a loving presence watching over you and loving you. The presence is aware of you and of what you need, and it reaches out to you, keeping you from being alone, offering you shelter and understanding. That loving presence knows you and loves you, no matter what may come or what may have happened. The presence is always there beside you, ready to help, no matter how long it takes, no matter how hard it may be. So do not be afraid, because love will find a way.

When I use spiritual metaphors such as the kiva or the Blessingway, images taken from Native American religious traditions, I am always careful to honor these traditions as being unique to particular faith communities. It is not my intention to co-opt them for meanings far from their place of origin or their original intent. I lift them up only as examples of the wisdom of my ancestors, the people of every indigenous nation who taught spiritual wisdom—in this case, the wisdom of blessing. The vision of a Blessingway— a path created by the act of blessing—is a powerful healing image. The Diné show us just how strong love can be. Blessing has authority. It has power. It can heal and restore human life.

LOVE UNCONDITIONED. "I will love you no matter what, no matter where or when. I will love you as you are, as you will be or have ever been. I will love you simply and honestly, without pretense or expectation. I will love you when I listen to what you say, seeking to know your mind, to hear your heart, to never turn away. I will love you when I disappoint you, when I make you angry, when I do not always see the world in the same way as you. I will love you and never give up on loving you, and I only hope you will love me that way too." So speaks the Spirit of love to each of us, in this and a thousand ways, offering love unconditionally, enduring through all our days.

Like you, I am a little overwhelmed by this kind of language. I have a transcendent image of the holy, so I do not readily or easily imagine myself to be on such close terms with the Spirit. Yet the messages give us some breathing space. They remind us that the love we are receiving comes without expectations or conditions. You are loved, you are blessed, just as you are.

FROM ONE ODDBALL TO ANOTHER. Let me celebrate your outrageousness, your odd quirks, and your essential strangeness. That's what I like best about you; that is what I admire. You not only move to the beat of a different drum, but you have a whole symphony. You notice what many of us never see. You find what the rest of us forgot we lost. You have bypassed the need to be in with the in-crowd and have created a community of dreamers. I, for one, honor your weirdest vision and your most unconventional idea. Without you, the world would be a bad movie. So, from one oddball to another, thank you for being what you are not.

The Blessingway is a symbol for the second rung on the ladder because it embodies a moment of transformation. It tells us that what we believe can change us physically. In other words, the Spirit's presence is not only real, but transformative. Blessing is the conduit—the channel—through which the Spirit's sacred energy enters into our lives. We are literally touched by the Spirit. We are healed, strengthened, and empowered.

In Native American tradition, we would describe this as receiving the good medicine. The Spirit's healing, the Spirit's blessing, does not change us overnight into something totally different from who we are. It works like medicine, slowly bringing us back to the fullness of our vision and energy. Little by little, day by day, we are blessed and begin to live in those blessings as we share them in daily life.

INCH BY INCH. You cast a longer shadow than you may imagine, for you have stood taller than you know. You have stood up for what is right so many times that you may not even remember. The choice to be honest, to speak out, to show you care, to say a kind word—it all happens in a matter of seconds. It is the turning point of faith, the instant of healing. You may not recall how often you have let yourself be that channel of grace, but each time you do, you lift hope high for all to see. The leaders of any faith are not crowned from above, but grown from below, inch by inch, choice by choice, one act of love at a time.

Once you accept the Spirit's blessings, you are walking the Blessingway. You have moved from faith alone to faith doubled through the power of the Spirit. You begin to feel more confident. You begin to try on new ideas and make new commitments. Simply, you begin to grow in spiritual awareness and understanding. You find that you are suddenly able to do more than you ever imagined possible.

> **PICKING THE LOCK OF FATE.** *There is a little Houdini in you. Just when life seems to have you all tied up with chains that can't be broken—chains such as illness or sorrow or financial hardship—somehow, like a miracle, you find a way to free yourself. You find a way out of the straitjacket of worry and fear. So, how do you do that? How do you pick the lock of your own fate? What is your secret? I think I know: you have a silent partner, the Spirit, who works unseen from offstage to loosen your bonds, to support you in your struggle, to finally set you free of your burdens. How do I know that? Because I use the same trick myself, the oldest trick in the book—trust in the power of love.*

The key to understanding blessing is accepting the idea of intimacy with the sacred. When my ancestors performed religious ceremonies, they sometimes wore masks that resembled some aspect of the Spirit. Wearing these masks, the dancers became that aspect. They embodied the Spirit as one of these healing forces in creation. Similarly, Christians speak of becoming one with the Spirit through the ceremony of Holy Communion. Both of these practices unify the level of intimacy between the Spirit and humanity. The

contact between us is complete. This is how we can understand the meaning and purpose of blessing: it is that instant
when the human and the holy have merged. This mixture—
divine power and human longing—establishes the link and
allows life to be transformed through love.

*THE SPIRIT STANDS NEARBY. I have a quiet word for any
among us who have had a less-than-perfect childhood,
full of painful or difficult experiences with parents or
peers that caused us to carry old and enduring hurts. The
Spirit is standing nearby, in the safe space we name, waiting until we feel ready. Then, with our permission, the
Spirit extends a gentle hand of love—a love that heals and
restores, soothes and releases—helping us to feel once
more the innocence of our hearts, the kindness of our
hope, the happy moments we have so long sought and
needed. This word may be for you or someone you know.
I share it as I received it, a free gift to any listening soul.*

Whether our coming into the Spirit's embrace is through
laughter or sorrow, the result is a profound affirmation.
When the Spirit speaks to you, that message overflows with
a powerful sense of respect. The Spirit's blessing is not a
generic formula, but a personal empowerment. The strength
to keep climbing comes to you where and when you need it
most. It is a feeling of confidence that grows because it is so
clearly rooted in love.

WHO YOU ARE. It is within you. It always has been. Since you were young, when the world grew up around you, when so much changed and became serious, you were never ready to give up. No matter how difficult, you kept going, you found a way. The word is resilience. It is the strength of faith, the courage of a life that has seen hard times but never surrendered to sorrow. How much that has meant to others, to those who know and love you, is beyond the heart's ability to measure. It is just who you are. It is within you. It always has been and it always will be.

It is within you. It always has been because we are all blessed with what we need to be the light in darkness. The energy and confidence are already there in our hearts. It is in our love. I believe the Spirit returns to this same point over and over because she is blessing each of us with as much love as we can handle. She knows our love is the fuel for the light we will generate. The more we believe in ourselves as agents of love, the brighter our light will be.

Many of us have been raised in judgmental religious traditions. We may have grown up being told we were sinful or guilty. Many of us come from marginalized or oppressed communities. We may have been put down because of our ethnicity or threatened because of our sexuality. Many of us have been abused as children or battered as adults. In all these ways, darkness has penetrated deep within our hearts. We believe what we have been told. We feel inadequate. It is no wonder the Spirit needs to give us an immediate transfusion of love and affirmation.

THE GOOD YOU HAVE DONE. "Look at all the good you have done, little by little, person by person, over all these years, with every helping act you performed, with every kind word you spoke," the Spirit says. "I know you want to offer a disclaimer, but your mistakes do not erase the good. Over all these years, you have been a channel of grace, a source of healing, a friend in need. You have acted from a deep sense of compassion. You have sacrificed for the sake of others. I do not remind you of this out of some sense of false flattery, but only to acknowledge a simple truth: if every bit of good you have done were a grain of sand, you would be standing on a beach."

I believe we begin to become the light that shines in darkness when we begin to believe we are loved. That is why many of these messages are so direct and personal. The Spirit speaks to each of us. She affirms us, heals us, respects us, and gives us a start on our journey to becoming all we were born to be.

SEEDS OF HOPE. "You will be feeling something different in the days to come," the Spirit says. "It will not be a dramatic change, but a slow and steady sense of moving forward, of seeing things with a new perspective, of having the energy to achieve what must be done. Old feelings of weakness will slip away. New ideas for you to follow will emerge. There are sacred seasons, just as there are natural seasons, and you are about to cross the unseen threshold into the days when life begins to stir beneath the surface. The seeds of hope are within you. You can feel them begin to take root, even when the land seems barren under winter's cold hand. Something different is coming into your life."

When love comes into your life—when you feel that love and trust in it—your whole reality begins to take on a different shape, a different level of meaning. And that is why the Spirit sends these personal messages to you.

WHEN IT ARRIVES. You will feel it. I believe when the Spirit comes near to you, even if you cannot see anything different, you will feel it. The presence of the sacred changes reality. It moves into the space around us. It occupies that space, fills it with a presence that can be perceived, sensed by us even if we do not see it with our eyes. The feeling is not dissimilar to how we can feel someone standing close behind us even if we did not hear their approach. Instinctively, we know they are there. Be alert if you have been praying. Be aware if you have a need. A loving presence, a power that cares, is coming to you. You will know when it arrives. You will feel it.

There is a power in words—the power to heal, to liberate, to beckon. Before we begin the work we are called to do, we must begin by hearing words that make us uncomfortable. Not because they threaten us or judge us, but because they embarrass us. The Spirit's word, spoken directly to us, up front and personal, is a word of love. Intimate, knowing love.

The Spirit tells you that you are wonderful, a masterpiece, made to do what no one else can do. You feel that love. You know it is meant for you. So, now you have a choice: Duck your head, shuffle your feet, and say, "No, that's not me." Or lift your head, stand up straight, and say, "Yes, I receive your love and joyfully return it with all the faith I have."

Ancient mystics of many faiths have described the union between the Spirit and human beings in terms of an ecstatic intimacy. What I suggest is a little less grand: I believe that when the Spirit speaks to you directly in words filled with love and respect, you feel it. It empowers you. It heals you. It prepares you for the partnership to come.

A PROMISE KEPT. The day will come when what burdens you now will be lifted from your shoulders, when your pain will be gone, when your sorrow will be no more. It will come to you as surely as the dawn, as a promise kept, as a hope fulfilled. Nothing will stop it. Nothing will hold it back—not your past, not your current circumstances. It will come—a gentle but insistent healing, a redemption, a fresh start, a renewal of the heart—and it will change everything. This is not a prophecy, but a pattern, for mercy and forgiveness always return to find us, love always seeks us out among the crowd, and the Spirit will never relent until all her children are safe once more.

You have been touched by the Spirit's hand. You have been called out by name. You have been blessed with many skills and with great strength. The darkness will begin to go away when you believe in the light, when you begin to believe in yourself, when you climb the Blessingway to discover just how strong your faith can be.

WHAT MIGHT BE. If someone asks you why you are such a dreamer, tell them it's because reality can't keep up with you. Claim your right to be a visionary, to see into the future with hope, to imagine what could happen if the sacred could just tip the scales toward justice. Don't settle for what is, but reach for might be. Let your mind gather the facts and let your heart sort out the reasons, but open your spirit to soar to the realm of possibility. The bland prophets of the status quo may think they own today, but dreamers like you slip past them to discover the way to tomorrow. Reality is just a rearview mirror.

CHAPTER 3

THE RUNG OF HOPE

THE FIRST BREEZE. Don't let the dark clouds fool you. They may pretend to own the heavens, stretching from horizon to horizon, ominous and commanding, a permanent shadow over our lives. But I know their secret: there is a world of sunlight behind them. One day, when the wind of change pushes them apart, that light will return to bathe the earth, to restore the vision of every person, to set right that which has been broken. Stand firm in what you know and believe. Look up and do not be afraid, for when you feel the first breeze of hope, the clouds will soon be chased from the sky.

In 1831, the world came to an end for my family—and for all the families that were part of the Choctaw Nation. That year, we were forced off our ancestral homeland and made to walk on a death march we called the Trail of Tears. Thousands of our people died. We lost our homes, our way of life, even our graveyards. We lost everything.

Everything, that is, except the one thing they could not take from us: hope. Hope kept us going, kept us climbing toward the light, even though the world seemed to be filled with nothing but darkness.

Third on the ladder is the rung of hope, because hope is what emerges when you mix faith with blessing. I am not talking about wishful thinking. I am not talking about miracles. I am talking about hope as a tool to create light, a spark that can suddenly illuminate the gloom that creeps into our lives. The reason we have faith as the tinder and blessing as the spark is so we can have hope—the first flame of light in darkness.

> SANCTUARY. In these troubled times, I know a place where fear and uncertainty cannot come, where confidence and hope still shine brightly, where there is room for every person of every condition to gather in safety and strength. That place is in my heart. The princes of power who strut their moment upon the stage may rail against the others— the many others—they seek to shun from the embrace of freedom. But in my heart is sanctuary for each forgotten soul. No truth will be swept away, no justice lost, no

mercy gone ungiven, for I keep them all here in my heart. There they are secure until once more they are released to join what I know is in your heart as well: an outpouring of love, a fulfillment of the prophecy you already read in these few simple words.

The Spirit does not seek to establish a spiritually intimate relationship with us without a reason. Some people find this relationship with the Spirit and then mistakenly stop there. They come to the second rung of the ladder and want to stay put. Once they feel the Spirit's presence in their lives, they are content. They stop climbing. Instead, they build a comfortable spiritual cocoon where they feel safe. They are sure this kind of unconditional love means they are among the chosen. Through their personal relationship with the Spirit, they are saved. But this emphasis—on a private salvation rather than a shared hope—is a mistake, because it cuts short the next steps in our partnership with the Spirit.

NO PECKING ORDER. Spirituality is not a competitive sport. We are never in a contest to see who has the most ethereal experiences or the deepest wisdom. Each one of us has had a lifetime of learning in the way of the Spirit. Every one of us has seen things, understood things, and discovered things that are both unique and profound. It is the collective voice that speaks the word, the community that embodies the sacred. We each take our turn being the source of what nourishes others. God does not have favorite children, and heaven has no pecking order. We are all worthy of respect and we each still have a lot to learn.

Hope is never exclusive. The love we feel in our hearts is not just for us alone, but for every other person who shares this world. We are all loved unconditionally. We are all in touch with the Spirit, even if we resist that pull on our emotions or deny the intellectual possibility of a higher power. We may pray differently, but we hope the same.

As members of the tribe of the human beings, we hope for good health, for a better life, and for a bright future for our children. Hope is generic. It is unifying. It is the unseen bond that subverts our exclusivity and our need to build religious walls around ourselves. If we open our eyes spiritually, we can see evidence of hope in every person and place.

SIGNS OF HOPE. The signs are all around us. We can see them springing up like wildflowers after the prairie rain. People who had fallen asleep are waking up. People who had been content to watch are wanting to join. People who never said a word are speaking out. The tipping point of faith is the threshold of spiritual energy, where what we believe becomes what we do. When that power is released, there is no stopping it, for love is a force that cannot be contained. Look and see the thousands of new faces gathering from every direction. There is the sign of hope for which you have been waiting.

One of the hallmarks of my Native American tradition is the understanding that personal spirituality is never lived in isolation. We may receive a personal message from the Spirit—one unique to us—but we never imagine this connection to the sacred is intended for us alone. When I say that after my prayers I listen for the Spirit's voice within me, I am claiming my personal space with the sacred, but I am never saying this experience is for me alone. Any person who prays and listens will receive a response. Their experience will be as unique as mine, but the purpose behind it will always be to strengthen and to support the life we share, not only with one another, but with all of creation.

The Spirit's vision always takes us down from the mountaintop and out into the world. Our personal relationship with the Spirit opens us up to engage with others. In doing that, we begin with the one thing we all share in common: hope. Hope is the catalyst, the tipping point where what we believe becomes what we do.

WORD OF PRAYER. All we need is within us: wisdom, courage, love. They were all placed there from the very beginning of our lives, stored away for such a day as this. Strength and insight, faith and vision, kindness and compassion—everything we need to survive, to overcome, to grow—these traits have been prepared for us, entrusted to us. We have the spiritual resources we need—the gifts and the skill. We even have the key. A simple word of prayer: Open my heart, O Spirit. Open my mind and my spirit. Let me use what you have given me. Let me trust what you have shown me. Let me be what you have made me.

My ancestors did not survive the Trail of Tears because they were set apart from the rest of humanity. Their exodus was not a sign of their exclusivity, but rather their inclusivity. In their suffering, they embodied the finite and vulnerable condition of all humanity. They experienced what the whole tribe of the human beings has experienced at one time or another throughout history: the struggle of life, the pain of oppression, and the fear of the unknown. Their long walk was the walk of every person who has known what it means to be alone and afraid. But they walked with courage and dignity because they had the hope of the Spirit within them.

Even in their darkest moments, they kept going, kept climbing. Why? Because they believed. And what they believed, they saw. In the harsh winter of their great struggle, they looked around and saw others walking beside them. They knew they were not alone. They knew the Spirit was in their hearts every step of the way. With that faith and with that blessing, they embodied the one force no oppression can ever overcome or contain: the hope they saw before them as their future.

To step over the threshold of our own fears, we must be willing to do what the survivors of the Trail of Tears did: embody hope. We do that by holding on to the third rung of the ladder with all our might, breathing in the confidence the Spirit has given us, then using that confidence to look into the future. What we see depends on what we believe.

OLD AND TRUSTED FRIEND. The future is not a forbidding place, full of the unknown and the uncertain, but a place as familiar as the guardian angel who used to watch over us when we crossed the street. The same Spirit that dwelled in the past, caring for us as children, is the Spirit of the now, caring for us as adults. The holy presence that helped us navigate adolescence is the same presence who is with us as we read these words. We know this Spirit. She is an old and trusted friend. Even in the most difficult times, we are not as afraid, because we know the Spirit is with us. We do not need to be anxious about what is to come, for the love that saw us through yesterday will see us through tomorrow.

Hope arises when we embrace a sacred reality. That vision is not a dream, but a goal. What we project into our future through faith is not just the wishful thinking of dreamers out of touch with reality; it is the blueprint for a future our faith sees clearly before us. Hope is not a wish, but an intention. Most of us do not think of ourselves as heroic agents of change, but if we have enough hope in what we see, then we find the strength to make change happen. When our hope is linked to the hope of others, we become even stronger. Hope builds on itself. It grows. The more we share in hope, the more we see the light, even in the darkness of the midnight hour.

NOT AN OPTION. Surrender is not an option. I cannot imagine giving up my faith in the real presence of a loving Spirit who is with us on this long walk we call life. I know goodness is there, kindness is there, compassion is there, no matter how final the triumph of fear may seem nor how great the power that holds the human heart down. I will not abandon my belief in the coming dawn just because I dwell in the midnight hour. All the more reason to proclaim hope when hope is scarce among the waiting crowd. All the more reason to keep singing, to keep working, and to keep helping the wounded to walk. Surrender is not an option—not for those of us who have seen the light to come.

Hope changes history. One of the greatest dangers we face is getting used to the darkness. It can resign us. In our personal lives, we can feel we don't deserve anything better than what we have, even if what we have is painful and wrong. We just accept that as our lot in life. In our corporate lives, we can feel we are among the outcasts or the marginalized people. As a group, we can feel weak and helpless. These feelings are real, and they deeply, directly impact us because they break the connection between what we believe and what we see.

HOPE IS OUR HOME. *One of the greatest dangers to the free spirit is discouragement. The lighthearted soul can slowly be pulled down by the gravity of despair, the feeling that goodness will never overcome evil, that justice will be subverted by power, that common sense has been lost in the madness of the crowd. In times such as these, looking up toward the open sky of the human spirit becomes liberating. There is no earthly force that can pull us down as long as we fly toward the vision that first set us free. When we refuse to give in, others will see us. They will take wing and join us. Hope is not only our horizon, but our home.*

The vision of the kiva is that even in darkness we embody the light of the Spirit. We are not lost, helpless creatures without any direction to follow; we are people blessed by the Spirit to see light, no matter how small that light may be. Through faith, we claim that light for our own. It becomes our goal. It becomes our plan. It becomes our hope.

When we claim hope for our home—when we make it the guiding energy of our faith—we transition from being scattered individuals who wish things would get better into being active partners with the Spirit, reshaping the balance of life toward mercy, justice, and peace. Hope becomes our goal. Once that hope has been released in the human heart, it cannot be forced back into the darkness. It is spiritually incandescent. The faith with which we see penetrates the shadows around us like a searchlight seeking the future. Hope becomes a force that will not be denied.

CLEAR THE PATH! Here comes the Spirit, sweeping down the fields like a rainstorm, racing through the city streets to a three-alarm fire, scattering everything before her, overturning sorrow and sadness, picking up the forgotten and the neglected, driving out sources of harm, carrying wounded lives to a safer place, thundering with the echo of justice, flashing with the fire of renewal. The Spirit's mercy rolls over the barricades of class and privilege, seeking out the humble spaces of the heart, clearing the path, shaking us awake with the power of an unstoppable love.

Spirituality is not an escape from reality, but a vision for how to change it. Therefore, faith is a tool for transformation.

It is not a private escape from history, but a broad and open path for many to follow together in changing history. Where we once saw only more problems and greater dangers, now—revealing itself all around us—is a plan for renewal, healing, and reconciliation. Hope lets us literally see the presence and action of the holy in our everyday lives. This is not an imaginary desire viewed through rose-colored glasses. It is the solid evidence of the power of love made visible in abundance.

SURROUNDED. Sometimes, in this troubled world of ours, we forget love is all around us. We imagine the worst of other people and withdraw into our own shells. But try this simple test: Stand still in any crowded place and watch the people around you. Within a very short time, you will begin to see love, and you will see it over and over and over. A young mother talking to her child, a couple laughing together as they walk by, an older man holding the door for a stranger—small signs of love are everywhere. The more you look, the more you will see. Love is literally everywhere. We are surrounded by love. The instinct to care is still within us—all of us—so much so that you can see it clearly just by standing still.

Hope makes room for love in the world. We can all share it, we can all believe in it, even if we are radically different in every other way. We no longer need to fear our differences because we have common ground. We can hope together—therefore, hope liberates us. It frees us from our fear of the other. It opens our eyes to see love all around us. It unites us and breaks our isolation. When we decide to embrace hope—when we choose to make that our goal and our message—we release a flow of energy that cannot be overcome. Hope is a light that darkness can never contain.

Hope is a decision. By making it, we choose light over darkness. We claim the power of blessing that the Spirit has entrusted to us. We understand that love was not meant for only us but for all those who, like us, have known the fear of being lost or alone.

Hope is creation in action. It is, as we will see in the next chapter, the raw material we use in working with the Spirit to create community. In fact, community is not possible without it. If faith is the first rung and blessing the second, then hope is the third: the vision of the Spirit we share as the tribe of the human beings. Long ago, my ancestors understood what makes us different from the rest of creation. They said other animals were faster, stronger, wiser, or more beautiful than we are. But the Spirit gave us, weak as we may be, the one blessing we would need most: vision. Vision is the gift to see both what is now and what is coming. It is the power to see into the future, to project into the future, to make the future.

ONE DROP OF HOPE. Free your spirit from fear, for that sad, old paper tiger is swept away before the rush of wind from the breath of life. What makes us whole is far more powerful than what seeks to divide us. One drop of hope can water a desert; one glimpse of vision can heal the blindness of thousands. Within you are all the great gifts of the sacred, the renewing force of your own faith, the strength of the peace you alone can release. What can stand against you? What can stop you? Nothing, cry the angels as they gather beside you, their bright eyes flashing with celestial joy. Free your spirit from fear, for eternity was the ground from which you were made and love unending is the fire within your soul.

Here is the holy equation of faith: We are as strong as what we hope. A people without hope, even if they possess all the wealth in the world, are weak and easily swayed. On the other hand, a small band of human beings can shift the tides of history if they have sufficient hope in what they see as the future. This may happen all at once, or it may happen over generations. Hope may be dormant beneath the weight of oppression. It may be small and precious, handed down through word of mouth, told in stories, preserved in ceremonies. It may go underground, a hidden light to keep the vision alive. So it was with my people for generations.

When our languages, our ways of worship, and our culture were forbidden, we handed hope down in whispers, in signs and songs, in secret dances under the moon. Until the day of liberation would come, the vision of our future could never be forbidden.

THE MOMENT DRAWS NEAR. With each passing day, with each uplifted prayer, draws nearer the moment of your next encounter with the Spirit. That encounter will bring balance, the healing presence of a gentle change, the insight sought and suddenly found, the help of others you never expected. The Spirit makes the sacred tangible. Your blessings will be as real as health and hope, centered in the places where you need them most, shifting the reality in which you live, touching those you love as if by your own hand. The moment draws near. The time is coming. Open your heart—it is already here.

When the long walk was over, and when my family finally arrived as refugees in a strange land, one of the first things they did was name that land. They called it Okla Homma. In our language, *Okla* means *people* and *Homma* means *red*. The American government assumed my people were using the name to indicate this was their land, because race in America was a color-coded form of oppression: white, red, black, and yellow. But for the refugees, as for the many other indigenous nations that suffered the Trail of Tears, the name had a much different meaning. It was not about race; it was about hope.

Okla symbolizes the tribe of the human beings. Homma symbolizes the eternal fire of the Spirit. Okla Homma is the land of the Spirit People; the land of those who have faith. This place, my ancestors said, is a community of vision, the sanctuary of light for those still suffering in darkness. My people gave the land a name that signaled to every other oppressed person in America that there was a place for them, a goal for them, if only they would keep climbing to freedom and not lose hope.

AFTER THE STORM. *The light will shine again. Even after the greatest storm, the light will shine again. The dark skies will clear. The waters will withdraw. It may take a long time, and there may be losses to count and lives to mourn. But life will reassert itself, slowly turning back to that comforting sameness in which we live without fear. Loving hands will help. Caring friends and family will gather their strength. The Spirit will dart from place to place, chasing the clouds away with the sunlight of hope. The light will shine again, no matter what storm you are facing.*

Hope is our message, our witness, and our vision. It is what we are called to share. It is why the Spirit brought love into our hearts. It is the tool entrusted to us to turn back darkness and let light shine into the shadows.

Hope is endlessly renewable. It is the self-sustaining, perpetual motion machine of faith. It keeps opening more doors, lifting up more opportunities, encouraging more leaders. Hope replicates itself in the human imagination. If we have achieved this goal, then we can achieve that one. Hope draws us out and brings us forward. It is the movement we feel when people are happy.

DANCING. We will still be dancing. After the long day's work, after the old problems are accounted for and the new ones are recognized, after the dust settles from the struggle just to live as we choose, we will still be up on our feet when the music starts. They cannot keep us down. Sure, we are tired. Yes, we have been disappointed. But there is something extra in us other people did not expect: the sound of angels singing in our ears. What we do, we do for no other reason than that we love life too much to do otherwise. We have the Spirit within us. When the day is done, we will still be dancing.

As people of faith, any faith, you and I are called to join the dance of hope. We are called out of our own private worlds, out of our own fears and prejudices, to share the dance ground of life with people of all backgrounds. And the first dance step we take is the one called hope. It is the first because it is the one step we all know. Hope is instinctive. It is built into the human family.

> *THAT BREEZE AGAIN. It is so good to feel that breeze again—the fresh air, the scent of the sea, the hint of billowing clouds along the ocean horizon, out where the great winds sleep, rocking gently on the waters while the aging sun looks on with a sleepy eye. Fresh air, new life, a beginning—that is what we have waited for, looked for, but thought would never come. Ahead will still be many struggles of justice and hope working together. But for now, after so many days in the desert, it is good to feel that breeze again; that clean, fresh air from just over the horizon, where the Spirit stirs the air, swirls the air, each time she dances across the bright blue water.*

Hope is our vision. It shows us the goal of our climb out of darkness, no matter how long that climb takes. Even if our emergence from the shadows takes many generations, the vision of hope will sustain us. Even if the change comes in a moment of historic time, the vision will empower us. We walk by faith. We believe so that we can see clearly. We take strength from those around us. We build sanctuaries with every step we take. We know there is a promised land, a place for all people of the Spirit, a home where we can be free and at peace.

RENEWED. *Be renewed in your faith, strengthened in all you believe. Be blessed in your spirit, lifted up once more to do what your heart tells you is your calling. Be filled now with a holy energy, made young once more to continue your search for the sacred. All along our journey, the Spirit is there to help us when we grow discouraged, to support us when we feel tired. We are offered a cup of cool water from the deep springs of love. Feel the power of your own hope returning. See the vision that once inspired you glow again with the fire of heaven. Be renewed in your faith, strengthened in all you believe.*

CHAPTER 4

THE RUNG OF COMMUNITY

NOW BELONGS TO LOVE. We will not deny the dark clouds, nor will we fear them, for struggle is nothing new, because no hope is born without it. Why should we be afraid of the dark when we carry the banner of light? Why should we bow our heads when we can see the horizon? Come, let us stand together, let us walk together, sweeping away the shadows with our song. We draw a thousand more to join us as we reclaim the land of life and restore the home of health. This is the day to rejoice, though our task is far from done, for now belongs to love, and today is when tomorrow begins.

Once we begin to embrace hope together, we create community. We recognize that the spiritual life is not just about ourselves, but all those who share in our struggles and dreams. We are not alone.

Spiritual community is sometimes portrayed as a sing-along around a campfire. It seems sweet and sentimental, but nothing could be farther from the truth. A spiritual community is more like a labor union. It is a community of workers, drawn together by the pressure exerted on them by the darkness, who are determined to protect the weak and uphold justice. The community is tough and accustomed to struggle. It is designed to face the powers of injustice and privilege—and doing that is no sing-along.

Faith, blessing, and hope bring us to the fourth rung on the ladder to light because through them we begin to recognize one another in a new way. Not by the color-coding of oppression. Not by the exclusive religion of private salvation for the few. Not by social status or any entitlement of privilege. Not by any measuring stick of our own design. Instead, on the fourth rung we accept a powerful, liberating realization: we are all the same.

WHAT WE HAVE. We will walk together through this lonely stretch of road, all of us who have come this far into the valley of shadows. We will not be afraid or anxious, for we have one another. We have our shared strength, our common wisdom, and our collective memory to help us through whatever may come. We have the quiet counsel of our elders and the boundless energy of our young ones.

We have the depth of faith of many courageous hearts. We have the resilience and experience of all those among us who have passed this way before. And when the going gets hard, we have a thousand voices to sing, singing as we go along the twisted path toward higher ground, where the shadows will be far behind us.

In this book, I call us *the tribe of the human beings* for a spiritual reason. In the dominant culture, the word *tribe* is often denigrated to imply a primitive community. My intention is to recapture that word from the mindset of colonialism and place it where it belongs, in the organic definition it represents. Long ago, my ancestors understood there were many tribes, but they were not talking about other human beings alone. All the living creatures of earth constitute a tribe because they are all part of the same spiritual nature. Bears are a tribe because they all possess the deep spiritual nature of being what they are in creation: bears. So do eagles. So do wolves. So do buffalo. So do people.

In this ancient context, *tribe* means *same*: the same spiritually. It suggests being of one substance with the Spirit, because the Spirit is the creator of all that exists, the maker of all things. Therefore, the tribe of bears is of one substance, not just with other bears, but with the Spirit, who first willed bears into existence. We can speak of a spirit of the bear, because the Spirit is within the bear. In the same way, we can speak of a spirit of the human being, because the Spirit is also within us. As we have seen in earlier chapters, the Spirit indwells us, intimately blessing us for a reason.

In the darkness, in the valley of shadow, we can feel isolated and afraid. But once we have the light of hope, we begin to see just how many people share in our struggle. The first step toward community is recognizing our common humanity. Instead of seeing strangers in the dark, we recognize fellow climbers in the light.

The darkness foments racism and bigotry to prevent this simple act of recognition. As long as human beings feel estranged from one another, suspicious and afraid, then community becomes impossible and resistance to injustice becomes less likely. Seeing one another for who we are, therefore, is vital. In that single and simple moment of recognition—in that spark of light when we understand our shared identity—we begin to resist darkness. We begin to become the same.

> *IN THE SAME DIRECTION. I saw an older man standing alone by the side of the road. He kept looking down that road as if he was expecting a bus, but no bus stopped there. When I mentioned that to him, he said he was not waiting for a bus. He was waiting for a parade. He had heard that if you wait long enough, the parade would come back down your street. He had missed it before and he did not want to miss it again. I looked at him. He was*

*different from me. Different color. Different religion. He
looked a little grubby and he had an accent, but I decided
it didn't matter. He was a person. I was a person. He
needed a parade. I needed a parade. He had hope. I had
hope. So I waited beside him, looking down the street in
the same direction. And the minute I did, we both heard
music in the distance.*

One of the greatest challenges we face in our ascent to
freedom is the fear of diversity. Throughout the centuries,
oppressive cultures have invented scores of ways to pretend human beings are fundamentally different. They have
invented the concept of race. They have developed elabo-
rate caste systems. They have engineered class distinctions.
They have economically separated people by gender. They
have practiced religious exclusivity and intolerance. The list
goes on, but the results have been the same. Humanity has
remained fractured along imaginary fault lines created by
fear and perpetrated for social control and domination.

In the kiva, we begin overcoming this fear. We begin
to see the deeper truth of our own humanity. The higher
we climb on the ladder, the more we realize the reality of
our own existence. We are not different; we are the same.
The light exposes these false divisions and helps us recognize one another for what we are: brothers and sisters in the
great tribe of the human beings.

TRUE VISION. It is an optical illusion, this idea that there is such a great distance between us. Those of us who are of different colors or cultures or traditions or politics, we have listened so long to all the reasons we are apart that we have forgotten we are standing side by side. If by the healing of faith our vision could be true, cleared of the blindness of ideology or fear or superstition, we would see other human beings as much in need of love as we are, as much in need of food and shelter, as much in need of hope for honest work and peace for their children. The great revolution will come when we cease to see through lenses we are trained to wear and look for ourselves into the face of the Spirit's single creation.

The acceptance of diversity is the beginning of unity—and of community. Spiritual community is never exclusive. It is made up by people who are different from one another, but who recognize their common humanity. The key is in understanding the distinction between individualism and individuality. Colonialism brought to America the idea of individualism. The rugged individualist was the pioneer who saw what he wanted and took it. In this reality, community was rooted in convenience, and it became an endless competition between individuals who came together or broke apart for any number of economic or political reasons.

In contrast, my ancestors believed in individuality: each person's right to be uniquely who they are but never to be ostracized or isolated from their collective community. Diversity, therefore, was preserved in the heart of unity.

LOVE IS A SONG. Love knows no color, no class or culture, no nationality or religion, but exists in all the above. Love exists in the hearts of the weak and the strong, the mighty and the humble. It flows out into isolated villages and into the streets of great cities, moving among the young and old alike, taking expression in a thousand ways— the touch, the look, the feel of an emotion deeper than those who have it, enduring, fragile, and perfect in blessing. Love is the inheritance of mystery that we leave to the universe—the proof that consciousness is more than chemicals and fire, but rather a song that sings the why and how of all creation. Love sings it now and will sing it until the end of time.

Entering spiritual community does not require us to give up anything we believe. It does not mean we have to lose our own identity. We can still be Christian or Buddhist or Muslim. We can still be politically liberal or conservative. We can still practice our own traditions and values. It only means we have to accord that same right to others and we have to defend that right to ensure justice for all. Standing up for one another, no matter our differences, is how spiritual community works.

> **WILD FAITH.** *We are a wild bunch of believers, those of us who break the rules for a good cause. We practice undisciplined smiling when others preach doom and gloom. We are out back helping to feed the neighbors while others are up front talking about why the neighbors are not hungry. There is more than a method to our madness of love. We are not disrespectful of somber predictions for our shared future, but unwilling to let resignation be our best shot. We are joyfully insistent on the alternative of hope. We are unapologetically committed to trusting in something bigger than ourselves. We are wild because faith is wild when it is untamed by the fences of fear.*

There is a kind of exuberant joy in the liberation of community. This rung on the ladder to the light has room for all. Once we recognize that we do not have to be self-protective and afraid—once we inhabit a family full of diversity and difference—then we become empowered. The light helps us not only to recognize one another, but to work together. We feel stronger. We feel ready to face the darkness and push back.

WE WILL NOT PRETEND. We will not give up, go away, or be quiet. We will remain here, standing in the way of the victory parade, spoiling the photo op, embarrassing the guests at the penthouse party. We will continue to resist oppression. We will not allow society to return to a culture of closets. We will not pretend this is the best of all possible ecological worlds. We do not think we have all the answers, but we will never stop asking questions. We are the quiet people of the center, the struggling people of the margins, the determined survivors from the bottom rung. We are the new community of faith, unified by a shared vision of human dignity, strengthened by a common belief in the power of love. Until history moves toward justice, we will not give up, go away, or be quiet.

Once we recognize one another as related, as members of the same family, we cannot rest easy as long as we see some members of our family being treated unfairly. Our social action does not come from a desire to be politically correct, but from an awareness that when one suffers, we all suffer.

Community is how we respond to injustice. It is our unified reaction to oppression or bigotry. Community is how we hold diversity in equilibrium. It is how we maintain balance. Doing this is not easy. It requires our commitment and our willingness to learn. A diverse community is a constant learning experience. It is a school of awareness, a center of intellectual exchange.

> SMALL HISTORIES. *We are as wise as our willingness to learn. We are as strong as our willingness to believe. We are as kind as our willingness to share. Free will—that's what generations of sages have called it—is the ability of human beings to choose their response to experience. We are not spiritual puppets. There are no strings. We have the ability to shape and create our own reality. What we do can alter the course of history, especially the small histories we all inhabit as our everyday lives. We are able, if we are willing, to be partners in creation. By our own decisions, we are able to work with the Spirit in writing a story that has no ending.*

Halfway up the ladder to the light, we are called to make an affirmation of faith: Do we believe we are all the same? Do we believe we are all in this climb together? Are we willing to help one another, no matter what it takes, to reach our goal together?

If our answer arises from the rugged individualism of imaginary differences and endless competition, then we will never move beyond the idea of communities as chessboards on which we all play for our own advantage. But if our response comes from the individuality expressed in diversity, then our communities will be extended families, sources of shared support, and bearers of a common vision.

Change is not easy. It can be difficult, painful, and even dangerous. The simplified solution is oppression—a return to the old pecking orders and caste systems. For centuries, we have suffered that smothering social dogma. We have seen its results in the misery of greed, exploitation, and war. On the other hand, with the vision of unity in diversity, with a willingness to learn, and with faith in the Spirit, we can confront the old agendas of colonialism and offer one another a brighter future.

AS LONG AS IT TAKES. We are here for the long haul, we veterans of the sacred struggle. We may be a little dirty and a little tired and a little outnumbered by the powers against which we contend. But we are not giving up, running away, or seeking to surrender. We are here for a cause we will not abandon, for people we will not abandon. The hungry and the homeless, the refugee and the immigrant, the poor and the forgotten, the innocent and the vulnerable—we make this stand for them, and we will not betray their hopes. We are here for the earth, for the life of creation, and for the future of our children, and we are not going anywhere until justice is secure. We are here for as long as it takes.

In the end, our hope is only as strong as our community. Many times we may be tempted to withdraw from the messy demands of living alongside others. We may find it easier to maintain a private spirituality or to simply disappear into the exclusive claims of a particular religion. Both of those options are far less difficult than hanging in there with a bunch of other human beings who are diverse and hurting.

Choosing to stand together can be hard, especially for some of us who have tried and have been disappointed by the effort. And yet, unless we make that effort, we will remain isolated and vulnerable when darkness comes into our lives.

DESPITE RELIGION. I have been thinking about how many people remain faithful seekers despite having had a bad experience in organized religion. Like many others, I have some sad and strange stories to tell about my relationship to the institution, so I know the depth to which people can be hurt. I honor those people for their witness and support them in their search for recovery. Most of all, I celebrate the tenacity of their faith. They remind me that faith can be found despite religion as well as because of it. Our journeys are varied, our experiences unique, but the home we seek is the same: a place of trust, a place of welcome, a place of respect.

A place of trust, welcome, and respect—that is the community we seek. It is not a community of one. It is not a gated community for a few of us who believe that we alone have found the truth. It is a wide, open community, welcoming to every human being. It is an environment of trust in which people can feel safe, especially if they have escaped from oppression or exploitation. It is a community built on mutual respect as much as on self-respect. It is a community of seekers, but it is also a community of activists.

THE MANY DENIED. The time draws near when those bent by oppression will straighten themselves in pride once more, rise up to claim their long-withheld birthright, and bring the light of justice to a darkened land. This is not prophecy, but history—the lessons of a thousand generations who have seen the pendulum swing from the powerful few who seek to rule to the many denied too long the freedom they deserve. We cannot go back. Diversity is destiny. Equality is our shared vision. The earth is our common care. No force can bury what lives nor silence what speaks in so many hearts that hold the human spirit sacred.

We cannot go back into darkness. We know diversity is our destiny. If we live into it, we will find peace and freedom. We will become the light.

We cannot overcome darkness alone. We are meant to be not a solo act, but a choir. Diverse voices can sing together. Different visions can be unified for the common good. A variety of visions can reveal a single goal. Diversity is our strength. When enough of us come together, no matter how weak we may have felt when we were alone, we become a light so bright that no darkness can hide it. We become an inspiration to others. We become their hope.

SING COMFORT. Sing on, choir of faith, and let your voices resound throughout the world. Sing on, songs of a sacred promise, songs of an enduring love, songs of eternal mercy. Let those anthems fill the air, ringing like bells for all to hear. Sing comfort, sing courage, sing the defiant heart of faith that lifts the human spirit on sounds of joy to reach the high country of hope. Sing on, choir of faith, until you wrap this weary old world in the arms of peace, singing it to sleep beneath the ever-watchful eye. We need your beauty now more than we can say—so sing on, dear friends, sing on.

CHAPTER 5

THE RUNG OF ACTION

WHAT WE SAY, WHAT WE DO. I saw a poster long ago that I still remember. It depicted an Apache man looking straight ahead with regal determination. The poster's tagline said: "We need less thunder in the mouth and more lightning in the hand." That made me smile. Like you, I live in an age in which we confuse truth with thunder and action with lightning. What we say and what we do drift apart. What we hear we do not believe. What we see we do not trust. Who we are we do not know.

So far, we have climbed four rungs on the ladder to the light. We began with faith, the first rung, which opens our hearts to the reality of the Spirit. That openness makes room for the Spirit to work with us through blessing, the second rung, the infusion of love that allows us to do what we would otherwise not be able to do. The third rung in our climb is hope, which faith and blessing produce in any human heart. Hope gives birth to community, the fourth rung, the united family growing in strength by growing in diversity. Now we come to the fifth rung, which challenges us to put what we have learned to work.

Spiritual books are often like meringue on a pie. They are fluffy, sweet, and decorative, but not substantial. They don't meet our needs because they never answer the hard question: But how will it work? Saying we have faith, blessing, hope, and community sounds good. But what do these things actually *do*? Spirituality can have many poetic images but few pragmatic applications, so I want to hold my own feet to the fire. I began this book with a story about my visit to a comfortable New England parish. I want to go back there and answer some difficult questions.

THE LIGHT BEYOND THE HILL. Your spiritual journey is measured not by how many answers you have accumulated, but by how many questions you have confronted. We are not gods who must know everything, gatekeepers to truth—we are seekers who look for the truth where it may be most difficult to find. Our wisdom is not in what we know, but in what we wonder. The light beyond the hill calls us to leave the shadows, even if the shadows were our pride and our possession.

When I asked the good people of the parish to name one cultural institution in which they still had complete confidence, they were silent. They were silent because they were unsure. They had lost faith in the classic sources of our shared confidence.

They did not have faith in our educational, economic, judicial, political, or health care systems. They had begun to doubt religious institutions. They felt our natural environment—the systems of the earth—were failing as well. In every category of confidence they were in crisis. They did not believe in the categories of leadership that once held their loyalty. They did not think the government would ultimately do anything to seriously alter their reality, a reality I describe in this book as darkness.

I want to change that perception. Even if we do face darkness, that is never the final word. There is something we can do. We can regain our confidence, both in ourselves and in one another. We can hope. We can join together in community. We can learn from other cultures and grow stronger. In the end, we can overcome the darkness and shift the pendulum of history toward the light. But I do not want to leave it at that. I do not want to allow myself to imagine that by just saying everything will be all right I have accomplished what I set out to do.

MAKERS. *If we know anything about the Spirit, it is this: she likes to make things. Vast galaxies spinning countless stars like a pinwheel, endless planets with* mountains and valleys of every shape and size, tiny cells hidden in land frozen for a thousand years, and great creatures swimming silently in distant seas. What the Spirit thinks comes to be; what she dreams, happens; when she speaks, matter changes shape and energy crackles through the open places of our lives. She is the maker of all things, and she calls each one of us to share her image. Not to be complacent. Not to sit idle in the heart of change, but to take up our tools and make tomorrow happen.

I need to explain how hope works. I need to bring my vision down to earth and describe what it will do when it gets its hands dirty working in the real world. I need to ask myself how what I have said in this book could begin to restore our hope in those same public institutions that produced only silence in that parish hall long ago.

So I will consider once more the questions we raised there about our cultural institutions and how we see them in this time of darkness. I will try to describe how these systems would change if we were living in a world in which the context of this book was the norm for daily life. What would these areas of life look like then? How would they be different?

I cannot cover all the ground we surveyed that night in New England, but I can highlight two of the most crucial types of institutions on which we rely: the spiritual and the political. I can let those illustrate the impact this book can have on how we can change our reality. Let's begin with the institutions that are the most foundational of all: our spiritual systems. In the next chapter, we will look at the political realm.

Today, many people prefer not to embrace organized religion. They feel religious institutions have let them down or abused them. The public scandals of philandering televangelists or pedophile priests only underscore this widespread suspicion.

As someone who spent most of his adult life serving in an institutional religion, I can verify that the public perception of our spiritual systems has eroded in many ways. Religion is often as much the problem as the solution. Consequently, in this absence of confidence in any of the institutional choices available, many people have either stopped supporting institutional religion or developed a spirituality of their own.

FORCE OF POWER. *The priest of power casts a long shadow over the map of our shared history. An arrogant culture disguised itself as a religion. Holy words of peace and comfort were transformed into a weapon. How often our religions march as chaplains to deeper agendas of control and acquisition. How pliable our ethics can be when bent by the force of power. Conformity was the creed; obedience, the rule. We had the chance to share the Spirit, to discover a new wisdom together, but lost the moment in the blindness of greed, to a hunger no faith could feed. What we believe is what we become.*

Fractured into competing spiritual institutions, religion still plays the roles it has occupied for centuries: a weapon in our culture wars, a cover for nationalism or colonialism, a power base for religious bureaucracies, and a constituency for religious demagogues. These are harsh images. Many of us who are connected to institutional religion will protest. We will say such characterizations are not entirely fair, and they do not fully describe the story of institutional religion. There are many good, honest, and faithful people in religious communities, we argue, and these same communities have done an enormous amount of good.

Yes, but as a drama teacher once said to me when I was cast in a college play: "Remember, if you believe the good reviews, you have to believe the bad ones too." So if even a small part of the criticisms of organized religion are true, how do we change that? What do we do? As always, I will leave room for people of other faith traditions to offer their own answers, but I will share my response as a Native American: we do the unexpected.

The spiritual system of Native America that I refer to in this book is a good example of disorganized religion. It is intentionally disorganized—that is the key.

THE SOUND OF THE SPIRIT. What voice do you hear calling you to the holy? Is it the chant of somber voices in the meditation hall, a call to prayer sung out over the city, or a cantor's invitation to enter the tent of meeting? What speaks to you? How does it know your language of the heart? We each have a spiritual sound, a code imprinted in our soul, to which we respond. Before we learned the lessons of our faith, before we were taught to recite and repeat, we had only a sound—a beautiful, haunting sound. We heard it, we came to it, and we stayed. The sound of the Spirit is the voice of hope. It speaks in a thousand ways, calling each one of us individually. The mystery is that we hear it as if it knew us by name.

Traditional Native American spiritual systems operate on an unexpected principle: it is not important to make sure everyone believes in exactly the same way. It is important, however, to make sure everyone celebrates what they believe together. This approach to religion is disorganized, because it is a matter of personal piety, not institutional dogma. But it is also highly communal, because everyone takes part in the annual cycle of spiritual ceremonies.

These ceremonies are focused on the one thing everyone in the community shares, even if their spiritual beliefs are varied: hope. The hope for rain. The hope for a good harvest. The hope for good health. The hope for love. The disorganized religion of Native America allows people to hold different opinions but feel spiritually connected through a shared hope. In this way, everyone is affirmed. Everyone sees themselves in the religious practice of the community, but without coercion or demands for conformity.

To understand the Native American religious system more clearly, consider this: Why do Native Americans dance so much?

The ceremonies I describe are all dances. Every traditional Native American religious calendar has ceremonial dances that must be maintained. The Green Corn Dance, the Stomp Dance, the Sun Dance, the Snake Dance—the list goes on and on, but the same principle is at work: the dances focus on what we all hope for together. And that's the point. Celebrating what we hope for together is better than fighting over what we believe separately.

THE ANSWER IS WITHIN. *It is all a circle, the ancestors said—an endless circle within a circle. The drum is a circle. The dance ground is a circle. The earth is a circle. There is no us or them, no top or bottom, no beginning or end, no lines of division—only a seamless embrace. The answer is within. It has existed since before time began, and it will be there long after the last campfire fades. For even if we are not there to see it, the stars will make their great circle of the heavens to mark the way home.*

Individual belief is interpretation. None of us, even members of the same organized religion, believes in exactly the same way. We interpret the meaning of our creeds. We cross our fingers behind our backs on some parts of the dogma and ardently embrace others. Native American spiritual systems take this kind of individual interpretation for granted and do not allow it to become the focal point for religion. Doing so would only invite people to argue endlessly about their differences instead of coming together to celebrate their similarities.

Organized religion is built on conforming to dogma results in conflict. It encourages exclusion. It opens the door to abuse by the institution. In contrast, disorganized religion tolerates individual differences, emphasizes communal celebrations of shared hopes, and draws people together. It gives them room to breathe spiritually and allows them to see themselves in the worship of the people.

In traditional Native American spiritual systems, people can still disagree about interpretations, but because there is no compulsion to believe in exactly the same way, these arguments almost never take center stage. Instead, dance takes that place in the community's religious life. Dance is at the center because it is both a collective expression of every person's hopes and an open invitation for people to participate alongside their brothers and sisters in faith, however they interpret it.

DRUM OF THE SACRED. The echo is still there. Go out at night to stand beneath the stars, far from the noise of the city, out to where the air is fresh with sage and the earth is still damp with rain. Listen. You can hear it. Listen—it is still there. The echo of the drum, the heartbeat of my ancestors, is still there, beating a rhythm of sacred sound. It is echoing from the sleeping mountains, echoing across the great waters, echoing in the forests and over the prairies. That sound will never disappear, for it is part of the earth. It is the echo of the first sound of creation—the drum of a heart beating, the drum of a life just beginning, the drum of a message you can still hear in the stillness of the night. Listen.

How do we do religion in the Native American spiritual system? We do it by dancing, because dance is more important than dogma. Dogma separates people, while dance brings them together. Dogma-based systems open the door for hierarchy because these systems need authorities who can settle disputes over interpretation. Dance offers different roles to different people at different times. It remains disorganized when it comes to the need for authority figures. Without religious hierarchies, abuse of the system becomes far less likely.

Imagine a society in which every person is allowed the freedom to believe as they wish without penalty or compulsion. These people would expect their neighbors to have a different interpretation. That would be nothing to worry about or to try to resolve. Instead, the focus would be on communal activities that gathered people around their shared hopes and that expressed those hopes in ways that invited the whole community to participate.

The fifth rung on the ladder to the light challenges us to take action. To do something together. To keep climbing. But our ability to work together has been weighed down by the demand for conformity. Organized religion has told us we must first agree before we can cooperate. And because these religions have competing truth claims, the chances for agreement are small. Action grinds to a halt. Not much gets done.

THERE IS NO STRANGER. *Who would you not feed if they came to you hungry? Who would you turn away if they were in need? There is no stranger at your door, only a reflection of yourself, standing there, hands outstretched, in a different time, at a different door. Hospitality is not charity, but recognition. Hospitality is the endless déjà vu of the sacred—we have all been here before. We have all felt this way before. We are as alike as hunger. When we give to one another, we acknowledge that we are not strangers, never strangers, but a family in search of itself, a tribe gone wandering now finding its way home. When we feed one another, we feed ourselves.*

The disorganized religion of Native American tradition offers a different model. It tells us there is a great deal we can do together. The metaphor of sacred dance embodies that invitation. It illustrates a community engaged in spiritual action, in movement and in step with one another, even if the dancers' religious interpretations are different. The important thing is to get out on the dance ground together. To stand up and walk out into the open space between us. To acknowledge our common hopes. To learn to celebrate even in the midst of disagreement. But even if my own imagination does not do justice to the possibility, one thing is certain: if we are going to regain confidence in our spiritual systems, then we are going to have to break those systems free of the gridlock of competing truth claims. As long as we remain in our bunkers of religious dogma, refusing to find common ground, we will be mired in darkness.

THE LAND BETWEEN US. Religions are not bunkers unless they choose to be. The holy name is written in a thousand ways, the search for truth is chronicled by a host of explorers, and the collected wisdom of all our ancestors is open to us to learn and to understand. The land between us is not a battlefield, but an invitation. We can be a people at peace, respecting one another, caring for one another, living in the dream we have for our children.

If we will take the risk. If we will meet the other. Come out of the trenches. Stand up in the open air. There is no war if there are no soldiers. Religions are not bunkers unless they choose to be.

The alternative I suggest in this book is not syncretism. I am not arguing for an "all rivers lead to the same sea" theological position; in fact, just the opposite. Native American spiritual systems show that people can retain their own deep convictions and practice their religious piety without interference. At the same time, they can be part of a communal system that invites and needs their participation for the welfare of the whole community, the whole tribe of the human beings. Whether that takes the form of actual dance is immaterial. The point is to put shared celebration, not competing truth claims, at the center of the religious system. These community celebrations would be designed to redirect the emphasis of our relationships away from what divides us and toward what unites us.

Right now, many of our efforts at ecumenical or interreligious cooperation are struggling. These moments are often more window dressing than systemic change. They are well intentioned but often anemic, a little like meringue on pie. I know—I have attended many events that show a brief face of spiritual unity to the larger community, but which never penetrate the surface to effect real systemic change in our religious attitudes about one another.

This must change. If we want to overcome the darkness between people of faith, we must be intentional about helping them recognize that they have more in common than what they imagine separates them.

Embracing a truly inclusive spiritual system as a community means more than having a few showpiece moments when members of a religious hierarchy stand together for a photo op. It means hosting intentional gatherings for everyday people from different religious traditions to meet, share a meal, laugh, and talk together—without the presence of authority figures.

LET THE PEOPLE SPEAK. Whoever said Native Americans are a stoic and silent people had never been to a community gathering at which decisions are being made. Each person must be heard, each person allowed to speak. And to speak and to speak until the words flow like the sound of water, a timeless current of experience, surrounding the speakers, washing over them; mixing them like pebbles in a stream. Let the people speak, for in their language is the movement of change that takes as much time as it needs. Let the people speak, for in their words is the confirmation of what we have always known and the invitation to know what we have only begun to imagine.

The fifth rung of the ladder invites us to take action. It tells us there is something unexpected we can do: we can disorganize our religions. We can set aside our disagreements to allow room for people of every faith and every walk of life to simply interact. Our isolation in religious institutions smothers our hope. We must disorganize ourselves, intentionally and consistently. That means rearranging our priorities as institutions. Serious interreligious community exchange needs to be advanced, with creative options for people to meet and engage without the interpretive presence of a religious hierarchy.

Would this mean putting Christians, Muslims, Hindus, and Buddhists together with no formal agenda or sanctioned leadership to guide them? Yes, it would. And give them only one agenda, apart from sharing a meal: They should share photos of their children. Tell the funniest story about their families. Talk about their hopes for their future. One hour of that exercise would be worth years of theological debate about who owns the Spirit.

CLEAR QUESTIONS. *Children have the clear questions— the ones so innocent, so pure, that you can see right through them to the mystery beyond. Why does the wind blow? Where is heaven? How do we know what we know? Questions asked in wonder, questions asked in curiosity, questions that were asked ten thousand years ago and are now being asked again, in the front yard or just before going to bed. Why and how, asked over and over again. Children are our teachers because they remember the first things we asked as the tribe of the human beings. Clear questions, transparent ones, free from any doctrine except that of amazement and endless imagination.*

Native America's ancient wisdom shows us how to regain confidence in our religious institutions. We have faith in what we believe not by talking about it, but by practicing it with people—and not at an arm's length, but up close and personal. We eat together. We laugh together. We cry together. That is the dance. The dance of our common experience. The dance of the tribe of the human beings.

If we worked hard for a generation at inventing ways for people of different religious institutions to spend time together, within the timespan of that generation we would see remarkable changes. We would see less religious prejudice. We would see more open-mindedness and understanding. We would see higher levels of cooperation among people of faith and, consequently, a greater positive impact on those hopes we all have in common.

In Native America, we have never stopped dancing. Even through the darkest times, we danced. We are still dancing, and we will keep on dancing. We will do that because we respect every person's right to hold on to their most cherished beliefs. But we also respect the call of the drum—that heartbeat sound of all life, that reminder of our common humanity—to get up and move together, celebrating the strength of the people when they are united, embracing the hope of every human heart.

ALL THINGS COME AND GO. Be at peace on this blessed day, whether it brings sunlight or storms, serenity or struggle. Be at peace in passing through it, doing what needs to be done, living as fully as you can, as authentically as you can, at peace in your soul. Know that all things come and go on the way to where you are called to be. They pass around you, they pass over and under you, but they do not define you or contain you. For your life is not an inventory of pains or pleasures, but a sonnet of the spirit, a mystery fashioned from and for eternity, a strength so powerful that it can afford to be vulnerable to love. Be at peace on this blessed day.

CHAPTER 6

THE RUNG OF TRUTH

NOTHING IS LOST. In the days of conquest, when darkness covered the land, the hoop of many nations was broken, the story of many people lost—and lost forever. The number who perished will never be counted, but their graves are still here. Their testimony is written into the earth. The wisdom of the ancestors is a mist over the valley, a cloud passing before the moon. The teachings of the elders can be heard in the rain, the message of the poets seen in the first stars that put the sun to bed. Nothing is finally lost. The ancient visions are within us. The old dreams are part of us. The steady rhythm of hope was never silenced. It beats today for all who would hear it. It beats within me. It beats within you. Life is still growing beneath the concrete. The sound of the earth is breathing beneath the glass and steel.

When my father was born, he was not an American citizen. He was a Native American, the descendant of a people who had lived on this land for thousands of years. But until June 2, 1924, when the federal government bestowed citizenship on Native Americans, he was politically disenfranchised. He could not vote. He could not hold office. He could not help to determine his own future in his own homeland.

Many people are surprised to learn how late it was in America's history when indigenous people were finally able to exercise any political rights. That sounds so un-American, but the truth of America's colonial past is that both Native Americans and enslaved Africans were denied access to political freedom. Their fates were determined by others behind closed political doors. Women were denied the right to vote until 1920. Enslaved men received the right to vote only after the Civil War, and even then, that right was harshly limited until after 1965. Native Americans had to wait until 1924, almost the first quarter of the twentieth century, when it was assumed they would soon become extinct, before they could go to the polls.

This historical fact, as unjust and unsettling as it is, has been largely hidden from the political consciousness of most Americans. It is an embarrassing truth for the land of the free and the home of the brave, therefore it is left out of the national story. Like many inconvenient truths, it is swept under the carpet of history. To see it clearly, it is necessary to climb up to the sixth rung on the ladder to the light—the place where that light is bright enough to reveal the true relationship between political systems and the truths they seek to either embody or obscure.

VOTING DAY. Voting day among my ancestors required a lot of cooking. Even before people began to arrive at the election grounds, the cooking fires would already be burning. Great pots of stew would be simmering while men tended the fire, children shucked piles of sweet corn, and women made mounds of fresh bread. When the time came for speeches, all those who wanted to be leaders knew not to be long-winded. They knew the people would be getting hungry as they smelled the cooking from the outdoor kitchens. The vote would be taken: a show of hands by all present. Then winners and losers would sit down to share a meal, while all around them their children played together.

Just as my ancestors used dance as a communal principle to express religious identity, they used meals to express political identity. Government business was conducted in the midst of a feast. My ancestors understood that the relationship between politics and bread is universal and direct. The whole point is to provide for the people. Politics is not an end in itself, but a means to an end—a social tool people depend on to help them fulfill their hopes. Like religion, the purpose of governmental systems is to provide a better community.

To do that, we rely on the women and men we elect to government offices to put the welfare of the people first and to do the right thing. When that fundamental expectation is disappointed—when the people we elect do not serve the community's best interest—we begin to lose confidence. We may even start to doubt the legitimacy of the system itself.

This is a grave situation, and it is one many of us feel we are experiencing right now. A gridlocked legislative system; leaders who obey voices other than those of the people they are supposed to serve; endless maneuvering for the sake of power, not for the sake of the people—this breakdown in our confidence seems justified. It may also seem almost impossible to resolve.

WHEN TRUST GOES MISSING. *Doubt is like water. It can creep into any opening; find any channel, no matter how small; and slowly erode any foundation, no matter how strong it may seem. Doubt whispers—it breathes its worry into the ears, playing fear like music as the sound of suspicion grows quietly in a nervous mind. While we can question anything and become stronger, we can doubt everything and grow as weak as a flower that cannot find the sun. What we have is only as strong as what we believe. If our faith abandons us, if our trust goes missing, then what remains is only a shell—an empty space where once great hopes grew like a forest and dreams bloomed like wildflowers along the road.*

The sixth rung on the ladder to the light is a break-through moment. It is the loss of illusion. It is when we begin to see clearly. The light at this level is too bright to hide the truth. Instead, it reveals it. Realizing, for example, that the United States withheld citizenship from its original inhabitants for so long—in a conscious effort to despoil them by denying them the right to vote or hold office—is a painful awareness for those of us who believe in justice. But it is a necessary pain, because it helps us confront the difference between history as truth and history as myth.

Like religious systems, political systems arise from a historic narrative, a national story, and the memory of the people. This may be the memory of an exodus or the memory of crossing the Delaware River—either way, the collective history of a community is both its archetype and its ideal. Political systems are who we think we want to be. They are wrapped up in our myths and our history. They are infused with our sense of identity. They are designed to turn what we hope for into reality. Political systems are fundamentally pragmatic. They have a job to do, translating dream to fact. We choose to put in charge of this machinery agents of the process we ask them to manage: they take on the mantle of the people, embodying our trust while they represent our needs.

SACRED VISION IS OUR INHERITANCE. Long ago, the maker of all things gave each tribe of creation a special gift. To the bears went strength. To the eagles, wisdom. To the deer, grace and beauty. The human beings had

> none of these gifts, for they were not as strong, wise, or beautiful as other animals. But they were given one thing that was special to them: vision, the ability to see both what is now and what is coming to be. Sacred vision is our holy inheritance. Not how strong we are, not how wise we are, not how beautiful we are—only what we can see through the eyes of the Spirit, for what we see is what we will become.

Native American leaders, therefore, were selected for their skills in dealing with the real problems of the people. These leaders were known to the people because they literally broke bread with them. They lived not in the context of power, but of community. They were not set apart or pampered. They were specialists in certain areas, entrusted with coping with a particular problem until it was resolved. Then they returned to their lives within the community without fanfare or recompense. Native American leaders, in the traditional sense, were engineers. If they could convince people they had a bright idea for fixing a problem or dealing with a need, then people would entrust them to do that for as long as it took—but leaders knew their positions would be temporary. Once the job was done, they would return to the collective, the extended family of the nation. This time limit was critical for a spiritual reason: my ancestors understood that the only natural predator of truth in the jungle of politics is power.

WHEN POWER STANDS ON ITS HEAD. The president in overalls, the princess in work boots, senators in the machine shop, judges waiting tables—how different to see power standing on its head. Power plays dress-up, wrapping itself in flags like dresses, posing before the mirror of its own reflection. Justice wears an apron, standing in the kitchen to do the work that must be done. What we do for the most must be what we do for the least. No labor above another, no one to rule—but many to reason, all working together, all working for one another. Can we even imagine it? Yes. When the promises pile up high enough, yes, we can begin to imagine it.

Governmental continuity was provided not by career politicians, but by the elders. The collective wisdom of people who had lived through many challenging experiences was valued over the rhetoric of those who may never even had the experience.

Like traditional spiritual leaders, political leaders could not be picked out from the crowd by how they dressed or by how they were treated. They did not live in special places. They did not receive special perks. They did not have special privileges. In fact, taking on roles of leadership usually meant giving away everything they owned.

When I was ordained as an Episcopal priest many years ago on the Standing Rock Sioux reservation, part of the ceremony was a giveaway. Unlike the European tradition of ordination, in which an individual expects to receive gifts, as a Native person I was expected to *give* gifts on my honoring day. The sign of my leadership was not how much I could get, but how much I could give. If I wanted to have the role of a leader—if that is what I felt called to do—then I had to be prepared to make sacrifices for the people. The giveaway reminded me of that principle.

> **WHAT WE GIVE.** *My ancestors told many stories about the first days of creation. Among them is a story of light. Long ago, Raven found the light: the sun hanging like a shiny mirror in the midst of an empty sky. Raven liked shiny things. He could have kept the sun for himself, but he decided to give it to the people. He brought the sun, placed it in the nest of the sky, and let its rays bring life to the dark world below. Raven gave away his most prized possession. We are not what we have; we are what we give. Sharing is the measure of our faith, the simple test of how well we have learned the way of the Spirit—not to have more for the few, but enough for the many. When you see the sun rise, remember Raven and give your light to others.*

Imagine a society in which there were no expensive political campaigns. No political parties. No special interest groups. No lobbies. No career politicians. Instead, those who thought they had skills to help with the community's most pressing needs would be invited to explain exactly what they planned to do. If they could convince enough of the community, then they would be empowered to do that, but without any expectation that they might be asked to do it again. Tenure would always be job-specific.

In addition, because their service was a sacrificial one, they would be elected to make a giveaway, which means they would not enrich themselves in any way. Like many of the greatest Native American leaders demonstrated, the most revered person in the community was often one who had few personal possessions. Their stature was affirmed by how much they had been able to give to the people, not by how much they had been able to take.

NOW IS THE TIME TO GIVE. *No greater love than this: to give all that you have. So, with great dignity, the buffalo laid down its life to feed the people. And the elk, the deer, the salmon, and all the creatures who made their giveaway so that the first humans might survive. Over centuries, their sacrifice has kept us alive. Their act of unselfish devotion to the circle of life has brought us this far. Now it is our turn to give what we have in return. We stand not at the top of a food chain, but at the center of a circle of life. Now is our time to give back life, to restore life, to free the spirits of all creatures past and present, to breathe once more the clean air of freedom. It is for this purpose that we were made and for this moment that we were given the power of change.*

The traditional Native American political system I am describing has a resonance with the democratic process we already uphold, but with a stronger emphasis on the ethical and spiritual nature of political leadership. In fact, the fulcrum on which all political leadership was balanced can be summarized in a single word: truth.

Native American culture had two characteristics that early European settlers often recognized and recorded: Native people were not afraid of death, and they always told the truth. Those were stereotypes, of course, but they were grounded in reality. The lack of fear about death arose from a strong spiritual connection to the ancestors, a deep trust in the love of the Spirit, and a sense of inner peace cultivated over a lifetime of daily spiritual practice. The importance of truth arose from a simple but profound understanding of what constitutes a civilization: no human system will endure unless it is built on truth.

OUR ANCESTORS' SILENCE. The ancestors stand silent. Before the clamoring crowd, the shouting politicians, the angry preachers, the dealers in empty dreams, they all stand silent. In their silence, they strip bare every word that holds truth hostage to the hunger for more, the endless appetite that fuels the machine we are told is our home. Let the ancestors' silence be heard in every heart, for it is the first sound of freedom. We have the dignity of our truth. We have the integrity of our faith. Even if all we can do is stand silent, let us do so with pride. For our witness is not more words piled on more words, but a vision as true then as it is today.

As we have seen, traditional Native American culture was not much concerned with religious truth claims, in a dogmatic sense. It *was* concerned with telling the truth on a personal level. The social contract formed by centuries of Native American civilization made telling the truth a core expectation for all human interactions. Speaking the truth was the highest virtue. Failure to do so was so egregious that it demanded the ultimate penalty in the political and judicial systems of our people—no, not death, but exile.

This degree of insistence upon truth-telling arises in our Native American cultures because we understand that without it, none of the community systems on which we depend will work. Truth-telling is the one essential ingredient in all of them. It is the prerequisite for any stable society.

SAY WHAT YOU MEAN. *Be honest in what you say and do—that alone could be your creed. Do no more than speak the truth to others as you acknowledge truth to yourself. See within your own motives as clearly as you see the intentions of others. Hear the truth within your own experience as much as you hear it from the world around you. Think with an open mind. Believe with an open heart. Let light shine into the deepest sanctuary of your spirit. Say what you mean and mean what you say, so that you may walk upright before the people, deserving their trust in every way. Deceive no one, especially yourself, for the honest path is the only way out of the forest.*

Today, from Native America's vantage point, tolerance of lies is the source of our dilemma. Once a culture allows truth to become relative or even meaningless, then that culture is in trouble. This is especially apparent in our political, judicial, and educational systems. Politics becomes the art of skillful lying. Education becomes the practice of telling ourselves what we want to hear. Justice becomes an exercise in power and privilege, not truth.

The choice between truth and lies affects all social systems on which we depend, but it is most apparent in the political sphere. If people cannot believe their leaders are telling them the truth, then the whole structure of governance collapses. Our anxiety, our fear of darkness, begins when we start to doubt what we see and hear. The Native American insistence on truth as a nonnegotiable for all social interactions is not a stereotype of the noble savage, perpetuated by Western colonialism. The Native American insistence on truth is a warning flag from a civilization that witnessed firsthand the cost of lies.

TRUTH DOES NOT GET LOST. Do not turn away from what you know is right, no matter the cost, because what you value in the Spirit is more precious than anything power or money can buy. It is your integrity. Be wise and be alert, for the practice of integrity is not as easy as it sounds. Some people will believe whatever they hear. Others will hear only what they believe. Some will say anything to get what they want. Some will want what you have no matter what you say. Some will deny what you can see so clearly for yourself. Some will distract you with a card trick of the truth. But remember, the truth does not get lost; it gets hidden.

The treaties made with our people were lies. The promises made to us were lies. The stories told about us were lies. The motives for taking our land were lies. The reasons for destroying our culture were lies.

Few societies are as familiar with the full impact of lies as Native America. We are very experienced with the outcome of institutionalized lying. Therefore, this much we know for certain: systems that do not depend on the truth become corrupt, self-destructive, and eventually lethal.

Climate change is a good example. Denial of the truth that human activity and choices are eroding the greatest system of all—Mother Earth—is already killing life on this planet on a huge scale. If the deception and misinformation continue, ecological breakdown will eventually reach a tipping point, a point of no return. This is not some romantic Native American prophecy told by an exotic shaman about events in the far future. This is truth told by a people who know the cost of lies.

In the end, our many social systems are interconnected. The lies told in the political arena will impact the judicial system, they will reappear in the educational system, and they will infect the health care system. Permission to lie is cancer in the body of any social organism. The more visible that permission becomes, the more acceptable it becomes in all spheres of life. Over time, it will eat away at the entire structure of a civilization. It will consume hope in a darkness that cannot be penetrated by any light of truth.

Telling the truth is not easy. It was not easy for my ancestors. It is not easy for us today. It requires a social contract that is based on much of what I have shared in this book: a spiritual commitment to something bigger than ourselves. It means taking the idea of community to the level of kinship, a bond of trust that cannot be broken. It means practicing what we preach.

TRUTH OF THE CIRCLE. *The circle is our sign, ancient and universal. It is the sign of our faith, the image of what we see each day all around us. The circle is both the shape of life and of time. The great circle embraces every living thing, holding us together in kinship, protecting us, bringing us closer. The endless cycles of time carry us like a leaf on the stream, spiraling out, spiraling in—the motion of creation revealing. Within these circles we find our place and meaning. We are all in the circle of life. We are all in the circle of time. No outsiders. No outcasts. No distinctions. No exceptions. We are all heirs of the same truth, the truth of the circle: we are the same.*

If the vision in this book were brought down to earth, we would have zero tolerance for lying in every aspect of our culture. And while that may seem like a fantasy to some of us who have lost confidence in our social institutions, it is good to remember that it has been done before. The proof that a political system can exist based on truth-telling is still there for all of us to see. All we have to do is look behind the lies told in our own history to see the truth of Native American civilization. For centuries, we developed an ethic of truth. We inculcated that value throughout our society. It manifested in how we taught our young, cared for our sick, elected our leaders. Truth-telling was the cornerstone.

It can be so again.

TRICKSTER OF A THOUSAND STORIES. Watch what happens to Coyote, that trickster of a thousand stories, who tries to find an advantage for himself, weaving schemes of deception, misleading his friends to get a little more for himself. Every child of the people knows the outcome. They learn it over and over from what the elders tell them. Tricky old Coyote tricks only himself. He looks only at his own needs and never the needs of others. In his blindness, he burns his tail or makes himself sick. His longing for a full belly leaves him yelping at the moon. Be careful, the children say, you don't want to be like Coyote, who couldn't tell the truth even if he tried—which he doesn't.

There is no special magic that made Native people want to tell the truth. It is built into the systems that sustained Native American life. It is a learned value. It can be learned again, and not by a few of us, but by all of us. We are a more layered and complex society in this historical moment than we may have been before, but the basic elements of honesty as a virtue are within all our cultures. Speaking the truth is enshrined in every world religion. It is an ideal to which we can all subscribe.

Honesty, like hope, can become a focal point for our community's regeneration. Honesty, like hope, is something we all understand. It is something we can do together. Simply insisting on the truth is a first point of contact for us to begin building a new civilization.

The truth about climate change would be a good place to start, but there are endless other places where the light we shine into darkness is the truth we need to hear and speak with one another. Truth will set us free. It will renew and unite us. It will ultimately heal us. On this rung of the ladder, so close to the light above us, the need for truth in our political culture becomes ever more apparent.

The anxiety felt by the members of that New England parish I visited years ago mirrors the anxiety felt by millions of people across this country today, people like you and me. It is an understandable anxiety because it arises out of our experience with political systems that try to hide the truth with darkness. Power—the kind that subverts the truth and feeds fear with lies—breeds in darkness. To prevent this injustice, we must shine enough light on political systems to make them transparent.

OLD DREAMERS. One day we will look back, a couple of old pros, veterans of the holy wars and the endless struggles of the human heart, to find our meaning, to discern our purpose, to build our sanctuary while we work the fields. And by the dimming fires of time we will talk, long into the listening night, and tell our stories of causes almost won, of visions bright and beautiful, of people we have known on our long journey home. One day we will look back, a couple of old dreamers, talking about the lives we lived, the truths we told, the paths we cleared so the ones we love can follow and find us here, waiting by the fire, wrapped in smoke and stories, the endless search of the human heart.

CHAPTER 7

THE RUNG OF RENEWAL

THE EXCHANGE. Sometimes faith is an exchange. We put down one thing so we can pick up another. For example, there may be no more room in our hearts for love if they are taken up by anger, or no place in our minds for hope if we are too full of doubt. As simple as this seems, that exchange can often be one of the most difficult challenges we face emotionally. The grip of darkness is strong. Letting go of what we have grown accustomed to, even if it is harmful to us, is not always easy. Releasing the past to accept the future—that is the moment that so often defines the present. Faith grows not only by what we receive, but by what we recognize.

One of the most ancient forms of prayerful meditation in Native American tradition is the sweat lodge. The lodge itself is a simple structure, made from branches bent

into the shape of a small dome. At the center of the lodge—
which is completely covered, originally by buffalo skins but
more commonly now by canvas—is a single fire pit. Men
and women each have separate lodges. Through a single flap
in the canvas, they enter unclothed, as you would in a sauna.

The sweat lodge, however, is much more than a sauna.
Once hot stones are placed in the central hearth and water
is poured on them to create steam, the canvas flap is closed
and the people are left in darkness. In that darkness the
prayer leader begins to chant, calling the Spirit to come to
the lodge to hear the peoples' prayers. These chants and
prayers go on for some time until everyone has lifted up
their prayers. Then the flap is thrown back and the people
emerge into fresh air.

The seventh rung on the ladder to the light is renewal,
which requires an exchange. The sweat lodge embodies this
spiritual concept because it is the place of exchange and
renewal. The two go hand in hand. The darkness in the sweat
lodge is like the darkness of the kiva. It is a womb—a place
of deep transformation. But that transformation requires an
exchange in order to take place: an exchange between the
people within the lodge; an exchange between all of them
and the Spirit, who hovers in the steam around them; an
exchange between the finite and the infinite. That exchange
is the moment of connection. It is the fire, the heat, the
energy, and the spiritual linkage at the center of the lodge
that brings about exactly what the people feel when they
step out into fresh air: renewal.

In this chapter, I want to make an exchange with you. I want to offer you something I believe will help us experience renewal, which is the breakthrough from darkness to light.

SACRED STORIES. Among my people, winter is the time for telling sacred stories. Young and old gather by the firelight to listen to the elders recount the holy memories. There are stories about famous prophets and heroes, about the ancient exodus that brought us to our promised land, about the creation of the earth, and about how the animals still remember that day more clearly than we do. Each story has its meaning—a message to remember and live by. They are told in winter because this is the thin season between this reality and the next. These stories are the unwritten scriptures of a wisdom as old as storytelling itself, as old as winter, as old as what only the animals can remember.

Let me invite you into the lodge of Native American tradition. Let me invite you to enter naked, free of any past cultural assumptions or prejudices, positive or negative. Free of past histories or hurts. Free to experience something unexpected within the womb of tradition. Free to share. Free to discover. Free to listen in the darkness to voices other than your own, but that sound familiar in their longings and their vision. Let me invite you to become physical in your prayers, to sit naked on the earth, to sit naked in the steam and the chants, willing to embody the sacred, willing to take the risk of becoming something new.

THE COMPASS OF OUR FAITH. Long ago, my ancestors created a spiritual compass. They designed a tool that would show them a path through time and space. They sought to connect heaven and earth. They laid this tool out on top of a mountain and gathered there to observe the mystery of creation. Over the centuries, thousands of my people searched for the meaning of life on this mountain. They followed the compass to find their vision. Each one of us can do the same. There is a vision waiting for us. The compass of our faith will point the way. The good medicine is within us. Our mountaintop is only a step away. Mystery is the door to time and space. It opens before us when we believe.

When I speak of my Native American tradition, I am offering an exchange. I am offering a perspective from the spiritual experience of my culture. For many generations, the indigenous peoples of the Americas have maintained community under the enormous pressure of colonialism. The exchange I want to make means sharing what they have learned about being a community of hope. I am inviting you to put down your own cultural views for a moment to listen to another voice—a voice that begins in silence.

LITTLE TO SAY. My ancestors valued silence. That is the room where the mind goes to think. The elders say it is not possible for people to make good choices if every-one is constantly talking. Wisdom is not measured by volume. If it takes an hour to get to the point, the point has already gone. Religious or political insight does not come with a glib tongue, a fast answer, or a sales pitch. Listen to the person who may have little to say but always has something worth hearing when they do. The Spirit does not need more than a word to make the light shine.

Renewal comes from deep within the kiva. It comes from within the sweat lodge. It is not just an intellectual notion about why we should try something new together; it is a physical invitation to experience that renewal firsthand. It is an organic experience, a chronicle of the human heart that stretches back through the millennia my ancestors lived on this land. It speaks in a language that is from the earth, from the creatures that share this life with us, and from the visions we have seen in the billowing clouds above us. To accept this exchange of spiritual insight, you will need to put down the idea that human beings are at the top of the spiritual food chain and open your mind to a world filled with spiritual presence.

EVER IN THE PRESENCE OF THE HOLY. There are angels in the rain clouds. Angels in the garden and in the sunlight. There are angels in every part of the natural world. They are the living presence of the sacred throughout all creation. My ancestors among the pueblos and the mesas called them the katsinim and carved their likenesses into cottonwood. Today, people may think they are only decorative dolls, but the reality they embody is far more important and profound: they remind us that we are never out of touch with the sustaining power that keeps this world in balance. We are ever in the presence of the holy, so surrounded by the sacred that we cannot tell where it ends and we begin.

The understanding of community, of kinship, in the spiritual tradition of Native America is vast and liberating. It is the universe in a kiva, the universe in a sweat lodge. Community extends in a great circle around all of creation. It includes not only the tribe of the human beings, but many other tribes as well, both seen and unseen. All living things are a family, and that family is permeable. The vision of our renewal begins the moment we understand that creation is not all about us, but about life.

DO NOT DOUBT WHAT YOU SEE. Last night they came again, the spirits of earth and sky, of wind and rain, of deep seas and tall mountains. In all shapes and sizes they came, from every tribe and nation: the deer and the elk, the bear and the wolf, broad-winged eagles and crows as black as night. They all came and stood in a solemn circle beneath the one-eyed moon and spoke with a single voice this message from the sacred: "Do not doubt what you see: the world is warming, the waters are rising, and the winds are coming stronger than before. Do not turn away, do not pretend not to see, but speak the truth and set the spirits free to heal the world, before the ice has gone, before the last tiger falls, before only the desert remembers the ones who once walked this land."

I want to exchange important information with you, because my Native American tradition offers a light that has been withstanding darkness for many generations now. Surviving in the shadows of colonialism, we have a deep experience of maintaining hope and striving for justice. We have passed through the valley of the shadow of genocide and emerged to help others face their struggles with hope and determination. We have climbed the ladder to the light many times: renewing our faith, receiving our blessings, maintaining our hope, living in truth and in kinship. Consequently, we are not a historic artifact of American history. Instead, we are the people of tomorrow, the people who have seen the light of renewal and never stopped climbing to reach it.

ELDERS ARE A PEOPLE OF THE FUTURE. My culture respects the elders not only because of their wisdom, but because of their determination. The elders are tough. They have survived many struggles and many losses. Now, as they look ahead to another generation, they are determined that their sacrifices will not have been in vain, that their children's children will not grow up in a world more broken than the one they sought to repair. The elders are voices of justice. They are champions for the earth. They defend the conscience of the community. We follow the elders because they have a passion for tomorrow. They are people of the future, not the past.

Tradition is not about staying the same. It is not about continuing spiritual business as usual. Native American tradition is the path to the future because it is how we constantly renew what we have. Faith is about making all things new. *All* things—not just a few. It is about transforming life in the kiva by reimagining it and recreating it until life emerges, just as our past reshaped to fit our future. It is about renewing life in the sweat lodge: entering into the unknown darkness of change, exchanging hope without the religious clothing we use to hide ourselves from one another, and singing our prayers to the Spirit until we emerge into a new vision.

THE ANCESTORS CARRIED US. They were as troubled as we, our ancestors, those who came before us, and for the same reasons: fear of illness, a broken heart, fights in the family, the threat of another war. Corrupt politicians walked their stage and natural disasters appeared without warning. And yet they came through, carrying us within them, through the grief and struggle, through the personal pain and the public chaos, finding their way with love and faith, not giving in to despair, but walking upright until their last step was taken. My culture does not honor the ancestors as a quaint spirituality of the past, but as a living source of strength for the present. They did it and so will we.

Part of the exchange to achieve renewal is understanding the meaning of ancestors. To some readers, it may seem strange that I come back to this touchstone so often. Why do I keep talking about the ancestors? Isn't that looking backward rather than forward?

Let me offer this invitation to a deeper awareness from my own tradition, from the ancient tradition of my own people, the Choctaw Nation: we practiced communal burial. For us, individual burial seemed strange, because it isolated the person. After living in the midst of an extended family for so long, a person's body would suddenly be put into the earth, cut off and alone. That seemed cold to us. Instead, through communal burial, they would remain in the midst of the community they had always known. Continuity in life would not be lost. What was would be transformed, renewed, into what will come. The thread of life would be unbroken. The past would move through the present seamlessly into the future. Death, therefore, was not a break in the path of life, but a doorway—a never-ending renewal of the whole community. Spiritual community that can withstand darkness exists outside the borders of time. Our ancestors in the faith are not only still here for us, but they actively seek to help us in every way they can.

OUR ETERNAL GRANDPARENTS. They are watching over us, all those who have gone before. They are our ancestors, and they have seen enough in their own lives to know what we are going through. They have survived economic collapse, social unrest, political struggle, and great wars that raged for years. Now, from their place of peace, they seek to send their wisdom into our hearts, to guide us to reconciliation, to show us our mistakes before we make them. Their love for us is strong. Their faith in us is certain. When times get hard, sit quietly and open your spirit to the eternal grandparents, who are still a part of your spiritual world. Receive their blessing, for their light will lead you home.

On the seventh rung of the ladder to the light, we are called to stand in the light of renewal. We are asked to affirm our willingness to change, for unless we do—unless we embrace renewal and strive to enter into it—we will not pass from darkness to light. Our ancestors survived because they could adapt, even in the most difficult and challenging circumstances, even in the face of wars and disasters. From the Native American perspective, renewal is about seeing the past as a doorway into the future. The more we enter into the strength of the ancestors, the more we emerge into the courage, wisdom, and commitment we need to live in the present. And the more we do that, the more we offer our children a continuity of hope in their own lives. Life's great cycles are repeated because they are renewed.

We do not live, in this life or the next, in isolation. We do not want to be buried alone. We live in a constant exchange: the sharing of our common humanity, the sharing with other creatures and with the earth, the sharing with the Spirit in creating something new. We are never consigned to remain in the darkness unless we do so by our own fear. Neither the kiva nor the sweat lodge is a bunker, nor are these things of the past. They are metaphors for transformation, for learning, and for renewal. And they are open to everyone who longs for light in the heart of darkness.

MATRIX OF COMPASSION. Here is a simple but profound piece of wisdom from the tradition of America's indigenous peoples: kinship is the spiritual cornerstone for community. Kinship is the sense of relatedness, the acknowledgment that all of life is interconnected and mutually dependent. Kinship bonds humanity to creation and unifies diversity into a matrix of compassion. It says we need and must care for one another, no matter how different we may seem. Kinship is the basis for an ethical society. Power builds on fear; kinship builds on trust.

Kinship is the core. It is the guiding principle that makes community work, not only among human beings, but throughout the entire matrix of creation. We are related to all living things. We are bonded to them, intertwined with them, dependent upon them, and strengthened by them. Our community is rooted in kinship.

If we undertake the project of spiritual renewal, we do so with a clear commitment: we are all going to heaven together. I state this colloquially to make my point to those of us who have lived so long in exclusivity and isolation. The spiritual renewal of which I speak is not for the few or the privileged. It is not just for those who have placed their bets on a particular religion and believed that by doing so they have a ticket to eternity. It is not even just for human beings alone. No, renewal in my ancestors' tradition is about the eternal kinship of all life, of all people, of all creatures, of all creation. No exceptions. No outcasts. No one left behind.

> BALANCE. *At the core of my ancestors' spiritual wisdom is a finely calibrated understanding of balance. Traditional Native American teachings and ceremonies focus on the equilibrium of all creation through careful attention to ethical relationships. They remind us that life is a matrix of kinship. When the reciprocal obligations of kinship are not honored, that matrix begins to crumble. Respect begins to unravel. Conflict emerges as life seems out of control. Balance is like telling the truth: it is not one option among many if you want to create a stable world. When you chase an extreme, you fall off the edge of hope.*

Kinship must be maintained. It must be constantly recognized, affirmed, and renewed. Therefore, balance must be maintained. The equilibrium of diversity must be upheld through justice, therefore mutual respect must be practiced. Consequently, hospitality is not just a virtue, but a necessity.

These may seem like simple principles, but they are difficult to uphold under the pressure of the darkness in which we live. Racism is much easier. Greed is much quicker. Striving for renewal takes patience, courage, and creativity. It takes hard work and sacrifice. Balance demands a give and take, a willingness to compromise and adapt. The digital reality of easy answers and immediate gratification can become a seductive path back into darkness. Climbing into the light means taking the risk to welcome the stranger, even if that stranger is a new idea.

> OUR COMMON CONDITION. One of my ancestors' fundamental principles was the spiritual obligation of hospitality. Any person who came to the door was to be greeted with food and drink. No one could be turned away. The reason for this was more than superficial. Offering a stranger something to eat is a reminder that we all get hungry. Offering water is a reminder that we all get thirsty. In other words, we are all the same. Those reminders are more critical today than ever before. As our society splinters, the ancient wisdom of hospitality becomes a powerful symbol. It tells us to remember our common condition. It calls us to act in ways that defy the fear of difference. We learn to be strangers when we close the door on our humanity.

When we make the exchange of spiritual insight and allow the tradition of Native America to speak to the darkness that surrounds us, we find a powerful new way to understand our situation. Without kinship, a nation is a nation in name only. It is a random collection of isolated people, all competing with one another, bound together by rules that often favor the few over the many. Consequently, the foundation for community is inherently unstable. The nation is always susceptible to struggle and injustice. It lacks a spiritual core.

Kinship provides that core because kinship means not conformity, but relationship—deep, spiritual relationship. In the Native American context, this means every person's right to be who they are and believe how they wish. It also means they are part of an intimate family relationship, grounded in sharing, cooperation, and mutual respect. It means being a nation without boundaries or hierarchies. It means being willing to take less so others may have more—not because it is the law, but because it is love.

TRIBE OR NATION. As a Native American, I find it interesting to see the word tribalism become common these days in the media. The term refers to the uncompromising partisanship that is fragmenting our society into angry camps of political diehards. The irony is that the original tribe, as we understood it, was a communal extended family that accepted diversity and welcomed the stranger. We called ourselves not a tribe, but a nation, because we understood that community can only endure when the essential cooperative unity of the tribe becomes the great family of the nation. Tribalism, from our viewpoint, means mutual respect. Without that spiritual center—without the ground of justice and equality—no nation can grow.

If we want to grow stronger, to become a real community of light in the midst of darkness, we need to exchange our fear for a different vision. I believe my people offer that vision. It has sustained us for generations.

PATH THROUGH THE STARS. *Last night, I heard a speaker say that as a child he was haunted by a fear of death, believing that beyond this life was nothing but a meaningless void. He has changed his mind now, but his early perceptions made me think of my own childhood. I remember standing outside at night as a little boy, far from any city lights, watching the Milky Way move across the sky. My elders taught me that there really was no death, only change, and that one day I would travel over those stars to discover another peaceful home. Creation is not a machine, but a mystery. Life is not a diving board over an empty pool, but a path through the stars. Fear is the void, not death.*

In order to receive the exchange offered by Native American tradition, we must put down the idea that the earth is nothing more than a vast accumulation of natural resources. Instead, we must see the earth as a living presence. We must recognize the interrelatedness of all life and begin to actively engage in protecting and learning from all our relations.

LAYING HANDS ON MOTHER EARTH. They call it a laying on of hands. In many faith traditions, when prayers of healing are offered, people place their hands on the patient. I have decided to do that for someone, and I am inviting you to join me. The patient is our Mother Earth. She is struggling to recover from the effects of toxic poisoning and exhaustion. I am going to intentionally lay my hand on her and say, "Thank you, Mother, for all you have given us. Be healed of all that harms you." It is only a symbol, but symbols have power. Please share my invitation. If every person on our planet went outside to lay hands on the earth and ask for healing, it might inspire us all to act, to work, to give for the sake of our Mother.

Accepting the exchange offered by Native America means opening up our minds to an ancient wisdom as subtle and profound as any religious system has ever devised. Native American tradition is not about the past, but about the future.

BEFORE THE WORD COMES THE THOUGHT. As so often happens, modern science and the indigenous worldview have come together. This time it is not about the environment, but about consciousness. In traditional Native American theology, creation began not with a word, but with a thought. Native wisdom taught that before we can

speak a word, we must have a thought to express. There-
fore consciousness, awareness, and ideas are how the
Spirit creates what we call reality. Science is exploring the
source and nature of consciousness as one of its greatest
and most enduring mysteries. Spirituality is exploring it
for exactly the same reason.

In the beginning of this book, when I explained where
these messages from the Spirit come from, I said they come
to me after I have gone out to pray in the center of the four
sacred directions. Like any good scientist or physicist, I ori-
ent myself to time and space. I acknowledge the four cardi-
nal directions as a gyroscope for spiritual reality, a reminder
that wisdom comes to us from every perspective, a ground-
ing in the connection between the infinite and the finite.
Native American spiritual tradition is inclusive. It offers us
a chance to renew our sense of community for the future,
because it tells us there is a way for us to balance our lives
in equilibrium the Spirit.

TIPPING POINT. One of the great values of spirituality is
that it connects our past to our future. Our ancient wis-
dom can guide us safely into the world of tomorrow. The
four sacred directions of my ancestors is a good exam-
ple. They understood that the physical environment
of the earth must be kept in balance. If that ecological

equilibrium is lost, they knew all life on this planet would suffer. Today, that simple but profound understanding is more important than ever. We are at a tipping point. We are at a moment of decision. Our past is asking us to choose. Our future is waiting for our answer.

That answer must be given through our understanding of and commitment to diversity. Diversity makes exchange possible. Exchange makes renewal possible. Renewal makes life possible.

The answer is in our inclusive community, our adaptable community. It is in our porous understanding of life. Native American culture offers this answer not as a theoretical philosophy of how to live, but as a testimony from the reality of survival. The result is a culture that survived darkness—unimaginable darkness—and came through with all flags flying in hope for the future.

OUR ANCESTORS' LAUGHTER. Last night, I had to go next door to tell the ancestors to keep it down again. They were laughing and telling stories, as usual. Endless stories, many with dramatic moments that seemed to require the storyteller to climb up on the table. Funny stories that brought the room down in a flood of laughter. Even the family dogs asleep by the fireplace got into the act by barking at appropriate moments. I don't know who thought heaven was as quiet as a cloud, because it is not. Our loved ones are having too good a time there to be quiet. They have too much to laugh about, too much to talk about. They don't even mind my asking them to keep it down a little. They understand I have to work tomorrow.

The seventh rung on the ladder to the light offers an exchange of hope. It embodies that moment when the entry to the sweat lodge is thrown open, when light suddenly fills the lodge, when fresh air breathes new life into the human soul. It connects the ancient past, the deep reservoir of wisdom from the ancestors, to the world yet to come—that vision of what we can do if only we do it together, not as isolated individuals lost in darkness, but as a liberated community of kinship, a creation renewed by the power of the Spirit. That renewal is waiting for us, just outside the kiva, just outside the lodge, where all life is growing and where the future is filled with the light of love.

RAIN LESSONS. When you feel discouraged, when you have a mind full of worries, the elders say to remember the lesson of the summer rain. The skies may be dark; there may be no sun, no light; and the earth can be so dry that it is cracked open and broken. But those same dark skies bring the rain, falling all around with life in every drop, a healing touch from heaven, a new beginning of hope for those who receive it. It is raining today where I live—drops of new life falling on barren land, falling from dark skies one by one, starting slowly and then coming quickly, like hope in the midst of worry as healing flows from every direction. Remember the lesson of the summer rain. Do not be afraid, but be anointed once more by heaven's holy waters, falling freely, falling for you and for every heart that is broken.

CHAPTER 8

THE RUNG OF
TRANSFORMATION

THE LIGHT IS COMING. Now the light is coming, running like liquid beneath the heavy shadows of night, slipping in from the cracks and crevices of life, restoring the dry and empty places, bringing new life to the barren hope of years long past. Soon the brightness cannot be contained, but spills out, pours out, to surround your heart with love, to bring you alive once more in an old promise fulfilled. Open your eyes and do not be afraid any longer, for now the light is coming—coming quickly, coming to you—and nothing, not even death, will be able to stop it.

Like many other Choctaws, I have made my pilgrimage to the holy lands. That means I have gone to the present state of Mississippi, or Chahta Yakni, the

Choctaw homeland. This is where my people lived before the Trail of Tears. A few years ago, I went there to go to Nanih Waiya and pray where my brother's ashes are scattered. He died early from pancreatic cancer, and being returned to Nanih Waiya was a way for him to have the traditional communal burial of our ancient tradition.

Nanih Waiya is a large earthen mound. It is about twenty-five feet tall, tucked away in a rural area of Winston County, Mississippi. For many people who pass by, I am sure it is not very memorable, but for someone of my faith, it is sacred ground. My ancestors believed it was at Nanih Waiya that my people, the Chahta Okla, first emerged from within the earth. Like the people of the Southwest, we have stories of the emergence. They have the kiva; we have the sacred mound. But together, we believe the tribe of the human beings began in the womb of the earth, then emerged to walk before the Spirit in a holy way. On Nanih Waiya, we first saw the light of day.

There I had a vision too. I saw my ancestors gathered around the holy hill, my brother among them. They were dancing, and in their dance they were showing me something sacred: the light is coming.

On the eighth and final rung of the ladder, we make our proclamation: the light is coming! We will need this vision in the days to come, for we confront a great challenge. The darkness around us is real and powerful; that much we can see for ourselves.

THE GYROSCOPE OF HISTORY. Frustration rising like magma beneath the social surface of the land. Helpless hands with little else to do but clench themselves into fists. Life like a bad dream. The monarch gone mad, and marionettes dancing in the halls of power. Each new day, another twist on a story that could not get much stranger. More than once, this has been the story of human history. More than once, good people of all persuasions saw the common sense of stable disagreement and the need for balance beyond the definition of self-interest. The gyroscope of history is not politics or profit—because neither will correct the course—but integrity. A cunning voice can call the many to serve the few, but an honest voice can rally the few to save the many before it is too late.

Through the chapters of this book, we have climbed the ladder of spiritual awareness. It was not easy. Our climb begins before dawn, deep in the fertile darkness of the kiva, the womb of our faith. Embracing that faith, that acceptance of the Spirit's presence in our lives, we began our ascent. Along the way, we received the Spirit's blessing. We began to hope, and by so doing we released into the world a power greater than fear. We did away with old prejudices in the light of that hope and we became a community of diversity and inclusion. We became active agents of change. We found the courage to tell the truth. Finally, we felt the renewal of our hearts and minds as we stepped up to embody the light we sought to see, but now have become.

> TODAY, I BELIEVE. *There are days when I feel so discouraged that I am not sure it is worth turning on the news. This is not one of them. There are days when I doubt the human family will ever live in peace and respect. This is not one of them. There are days when I think healing has passed me by. This is not one of them. Today, I believe in the final victory of hope over fear. I believe in the worth and dignity of every human being. Today, I believe all will be well with me through the love and grace of the Spirit. I may have bad days again, but this will not be one of them. I have a choice, and today I choose to stand again as a believer in the future before me. Some days, I believe I can change the world. This is one of them.*

One day, we will go to be with the ancestors. We will become the ancestors. When that day comes, what will those left in this reality say of us? Will they say we set an example for them to follow? Will they say we cherished the highest values of our people? Will they remember us as defenders of Mother Earth?

What we choose to do, or not do, makes a difference. Our climb up the ladder to the light is for a reason. This climb is for a purpose. It means we are able to shoulder our tradition, carrying it with us as we climb. It means we do not climb alone, but with every other member of the tribe of the human beings, without exception. It means we adapt to change and learn new lessons.

The light we seek is liberation. It is freedom. Freedom to live without fear. Freedom for human beings to live in dignity. When we reach the light, our climb is complete, but our journey has just begun. The climb is transformation. The light is transcendence.

WHEN THE SPIRIT PASSES BY. A hush comes over the garden around twilight, when the light turns to lavender and the first night breeze has cooled the air. A stillness settles on the earth. The flowers bow their heads. The birds come to roost in the trees. Even the little brook that runs beyond the backyard fence seems to cease its childlike chatter. Quiet comes to creation. I stand motionless beneath the rising moon, arms outstretched to welcome the arriving stars, whispering the ancient prayers of past generations, the vespers of my tradition. I lower my head in awe and admiration. The Spirit is passing by! Be still. Be aware. She walks the garden in her dress of evening shadows.

My brother sleeps with the ancestors beneath the green earth of Nanih Wayia. The light he knows is constant, because he has emerged into the future, where what we dream becomes reality. There is a ladder of light before us, if only we will see it. The link between this world and the world to come is real. It has substance. You can feel it. It is the tangible faith we have to put to use: the actions we take, the words we speak, the visions we serve. Native American tradition is deeply mystical, but also practical.

My ancestors would say this kind of close partnership with the Spirit is part of the blessing of kinship. This experience is all around us, if we are awake enough to see it. The vision the Spirit offers is not for the few, but for the many. Through her love, she makes prophets of us all.

THE OTHER SIDE OF REAL. You have heard the whispers on quiet summer evenings when you have been walking alone. They are the sound of the ancestors, speaking softly just on the other side of what we call real. You have seen the strange lights at twilight, like candles lit in evening rooms, beckoning people home to houses you cannot see. You have felt the touch on your shoulder when you were deep in prayer or bent with worry. You have known the energy that hums along the wires of faith, the presence of a power that knows how to heal. You have experienced the physical mystery that surrounds us, the mystery of the Spirit, the thousand tiny proofs that we live next door to heaven, waking up in a wonder we are only beginning to discover.

The ladder to the light is within you. No matter how dark the world may seem, the ladder is always there, waiting for you to make your climb. You do not have to be a saint to gain spiritual awareness or engage in spiritual action. Be only who you are: a person who cares. Be intentional about making your climb, one step at a time. Each rung is a lesson, an experience, a part of your formation. As you grow in each step, you become stronger and more effective in making change happen.

One of darkness's strategies is to make us feel too weak and too small to make a difference. The kiva tells us otherwise. This book's message is that every human being has the ability to walk the path of blessing. We are all called. We are all worthy.

LAND OF EARTH AND HEAVEN. Into every life come moments when sound slips to silence, when motion slows to pantomime, when the hard reality of this life blurs into the softer outline of the sacred. What is holy is not distant, but imminent. What you reach for in prayer is already in the palm of your hand. We are not mystics on a lonely summit, but common laborers in the fields of wonder. Feel the presence of the Spirit in the room where you are sitting. Feel the energy of the Spirit moving around you. You have dual citizenship in the land of earth and heaven, being both now and coming to be, being made of mud and stardust, being a child who is so soon an elder.

In this book, I have boldly claimed to have received messages from the Spirit. Does that mean I am special? No, just the opposite. It means I am common, because every person receives messages from the Spirit, even if they do not always see them clearly or understand their full meaning. The path to our liberation is in understanding that the spiritual life is not reserved for a few holy individuals or a particular religious community. Hierarchy and competition are not the way to the future. That path is for all of us, family of humanity, to recognize the dignity of every person who seeks a deeper meaning and a higher purpose. That is what the ladder of light symbolizes: the journey each of us makes down into the heart of meaning and back up to the land of purpose.

We may have different ideas about the source of our inspiration. We may worship in different ceremonies and pray with different words—that is a given, because we understand and accept diversity as part of our nature as the tribe of the human beings. Those differences can be the subject of conversation for another time. But for now, in these days of darkness, we need to be about healing ourselves from past conflicts and empowering one another for the shared struggle we all face together: the struggle to bring peace, justice, and healing into our world.

RISE UP, FAITHFUL FRIENDS. Wake up, sleepers in the shadows. Wake up to see bright banners on your horizon. Wake up to see your redemption coming to you, the answer to so many of your prayers, the fulfillment of your dream from long ago. Rise up, faithful friends, to shout

> the good news to the morning sun: justice has arrived at last, mercy has returned, love has won the day. Rise up, good people of many lands, for this is the moment of change, the time when hope starts to be real and truth begins to speak to every courageous heart. Wake up, rise up, and rejoice!

Long ago, my ancestors made a spiritual discovery. They learned how to live a spiritual way of life that allowed every individual the right to be who they were, while at the same time bonding them together into a powerful sense of community. Individual freedom and respect. Communal identity and action. The Native American experience is the experience of balance. It is a living example of how a diverse group of people can become a unified family. This offers hope to us in these troubled days, not as an escape into some mystical realm of shamans, but as a practical model for what we need to achieve if humanity is to live in peace and the earth is to be renewed.

We need to achieve balance: the commonsense, spiritual equilibrium that allows people to celebrate a personal faith while living into a communal vision. Each rung on the ladder to the light can be experienced and interpreted by every person who climbs it. The important thing is that we climb it together, and that in doing so we move in the same direction toward peace and the preservation of our environment. Rather than standing in the darkness, squabbling over our politics and religion, we could be climbing together to find shared solutions. Native American tradition and history show us that is not only possible, but relatively simple. It is as easy as saying a single invocation: I believe we are all the same.

SEASON OF RENEWAL. Awake, you winter sleepers, you tired and burdened believers, for this is the ancient season of renewal, this brightening time of green shoots and first flowers. This is the sign from deep within that life is never ended, that change is never complete, but forever making itself over, finding a fresh start. Life is rising out of the cold ground of the past to discover the sun waiting once again, a different way of being, but being all the same: stronger for the struggle, more grateful for the warmth, drinking in hope like rain, rising up to be seen once more, joyful and refreshed. The child is of a sacred spring, the slumbering soul is brought back to life, the great promise of healing is fulfilled.

When I was a child, I was surrounded by many images of exclusion. Our town was segregated into a white section and a black section. The town had separate schools, separate churches, and even separate public toilets. Our town was also separated by religion. The Protestants were fiery evangelicals who said they were the only path to salvation. Next door, the Catholics said the same thing, only more quietly. Even men and women were separated into their different roles and expected to stay there. Outside the town, Native American people practiced their own religion and never said anything for fear of reprisals. Although I was young, I could not help but see these distinctions all around me. I was raised in them, but I never accepted them because they were blown away by a single storm.

Oklahoma is part of Tornado Alley. Each year are seasons when thunderstorms turn deadly and great twisters snake out of the sky, roaring across the land with hurricane-force winds. But the winds are concentrated, pinpointed into a single funnel that can smash anything before them. They can kill in an instant.

Those storms do not care if you are black or white. They do not care which part of town you live in. They do not notice if you are Protestant or Catholic. And if you are in their path, you do not care either. Black or white, Protestant or Catholic, man or woman, you run for the same shelter.

I wrote this book because we are facing a great storm. The kiva is our shelter. It is for all of us, because we are all the same.

DETERMINED. *"I am determined to do some good today." That was a little mantra I created for myself when I was ten years old. I used to say it every morning when I first woke up. I was proud of this motto. It was important to me. I had forgotten about it for years, and I am not sure why I remembered it now, but I am glad I did, because it still speaks to me. I like the way it announces that I do not hope to do good or wish to do good, but that I am determined to do good. I am still determined. I know you are too. Let's do some good together and see what happens.*

Faith, the first rung on the ladder to light, begins with trust. In a world with so few things left to trust, we must receive and accept the critical invitation to trust in the Spirit. I cannot convince you there is a Spirit. I cannot argue you into believing it or prove it like a mathematical equation. All I can do is share my story, my message, and ask if there is anything in it that seems familiar to you. Have you been in the kiva before? Have you ever felt the darkness around you? Have you ever seen a light beyond you? Have you ever felt you were climbing? Have you ever noticed you are not alone? The ancestors' wisdom is communicated not by trying to convert you to an idea, but by comforting you and asking you to remember a feeling.

MAKE AND MEET OUR DESTINY. *Today is my destiny— that is a thought worth pondering. We know the ancient myths and stories in which destiny seems to be a scripted drama—the epic ending to the saga of one person's life, far grander than what we might imagine for ourselves. But unless we believe our lives are predetermined—with no free will, no actual choice—then we meet and make our destiny each day. We arise into it when we wake, shaping it as we live through the day, accepting it when we say our evening prayers. Today, your saga begins. Today, you make history. Today, by your faith, you give form to the fate your freedom allows.*

This confidence in the final victory of light over darkness is not for me alone, not for any one faith tradition, not for a private salvation, but for the whole tribe of the human beings. Like my ancestors, I believe we all came from the same place, the same womb, and that we are all journeying to the same place: the land without shadows. These are not metaphors; they are real. We all come from the same womb, and we will all reach the same destination. If we can accept those two bookends of hope, we can begin working together. We are related. We are siblings. We are a family. We have a common bond. We are here for a reason. We are going somewhere. We will take that trip together. We will arrive at the destination toward which we have traveled. Spirituality is not a collection of arcane and secret information. It is a simple and practical awareness: kinship is the clue to both our place of origin and to our place of destination.

WHEN OUR DESCENDANTS PRAY. *What a shout of joy there will be when peace finally comes, when war is only a distant memory and the last would-be tyrant has been sent packing, when the earth is a green garden beneath clear skies and clean waters, when the human family knows* no caste of power or privilege, when every child sleeps in safety and no family knows the ache of poverty. On that great day, amid the laughter and celebration, our descendants will pause to pray. They will say a word of thanks for all of us who kept their dream alive through dark days, who never gave up hope, who passed on the vision until one day it became the reality of a grateful generation.

The peace to come will come at a price. It always does. I do not try to write about spiritual things with the pretense that it will all occur without struggle. The climb to light is hard. It takes courage. It takes commitment. Most of all, it takes sacrifice.

Sacrifice is not a popular word in this culture of instant gratification. We do not like to give up anything. We want the luxury and the privilege to continue. Our sense of justice is that these same indulgences can be extended to everyone, but that is not going to happen. That is not the way it will work.

DEEPEST LOVE. May the Spirit's peace come to you like snowfall in the night, silently and least expected, surrounding your home, covering your world, keeping you safe against all danger. May it rest upon your shoulder like the hand of an old friend, comforting and supportive, always there without the need for a single word spoken. May it lift you up like a spring storm, fresh with the scent *of rain, clearing old hurts away with the winds of change, carrying your heart to heaven like a kite on the string of faith. May the Spirit's peace be with you like your deepest love: constant, steady, caring beyond the compass of compassion, to the depth of your soul, a stillness no power on earth could create or contain.*

I speak of my culture often because it is an alternative. It is a different way to see the world. I do not think it is the only way to see, nor the right way to see, but I do believe it is a helpful way to see. If we are ever to find unity in our diversity, it will be not through status, but through relationship. If we are ever to live on the earth in a sustainable and just way, it will be not through private possession, but through public sharing.

SEEDS OF LIFE AND HOPE. I have a small vision to share, one that came to me through the night walks we call dreams. In my dream, I saw a shadowy figure standing high on a darkened hill, throwing seeds into the wind. Once the seeds left the figure's hand, they turned to tiny points of light and were carried away into the sky. That's all I remember, but it is enough. You and I stand on a windswept moment in history. All around us is a gathering darkness. But we are not afraid because we have seeds of life and hope in our pockets. Our task is to cast them as far and wide as we can. The breath of the Spirit will do the rest.

When we are at peace—when we know the Spirit is real and when we are doing our part in unfolding justice and mercy—I believe our spiritual life becomes as natural as breathing. Every breath is a prayer. We will make mistakes. We will have some good days and some bad days. We will find ourselves on different rungs of the ladder at different times, but the axis point between ourselves and the Spirit, between the kiva and the light, will remain constant. The ladder will remain fixed and secure. We will go deeper. We will rise higher. But we will always remain in balance with the Spirit, connected by kinship with one another, woven into the basket of creation, made for a good purpose, and blessed with a reason to be.

PRAYERS ON THE WIND. Light on the wind comes the snow—fat, white flakes drifting down; white dust on brittle, brown grass; the air so cold that it stings. These are the hushed days, the quiet days, when the earth listens, for heaven only whispers in the silence of winter. Small I stand in this season, bundled against the cold, walking among the flakes, a single voice whispering back. Prayers for the lost and lonely, prayers for the hurt and hungry, prayers for peace and for the poor—my words rise as the snow falls; my prayers are light on the wind.

I have climbed the ladder more than once. I have come into the light and returned to tell others what I have seen.

What I share is only my heart; nothing more. It is who I am. It is what I think and know and feel. There is a land just beyond. There is a hope worth believing in. No religion or political party can claim that land, or define its borders, or control its immigration. It is a free land, an open land. It is the earth at rest and the tribe of the human beings at peace. I have seen it. I have breathed its clean air. I have heard its waters flowing to the sea.

I am betting you have seen it too.

JUST NEXT DOOR. I'm just getting home from a quick trip to heaven—one of those encounters with the other world, the reality that resides just beyond the range of what we see. There the elders gather to sing all night, to tell stories of days long ago, to speak of what will come. There we can listen to the sound of shadows, dream the vision of a fire in the night—smoke curling up to the stars, children sleeping in peace beneath their innocence. Then we leave it all behind to drive the highway at dawn, coming back to the loud world of confusion, but with a message to share: Do not be worried. All will be well. Heaven is just next door.

We must give one another hope by giving permission to speak of our visions, those intimate things we see when we look through the eyes of faith. We have all had spiritual visions. We have all glimpsed what we think is wondrous, beautiful, and holy. We have found our hopes suddenly incarnated. They are images that may last only briefly.

Spiritual visions are deeper than doctrines. They are untamed and unmanaged. They do not necessarily conform to any religious dictionary. By releasing them, by giving one another the freedom to speak in a visionary way, we open a channel for human beings to share in transformation.

My ancestors painted their dreams on their houses for all to see. It was their way of saying, "This is me. This is what I believe, therefore this is what I see." In the same way, we must be transparent in our own faith, willing to take the risk of telling others what the Spirit has shown us through a lifetime of our experience.

RUN BAREFOOT. *Our minds were not made to be squeezed into shape, like feet into shoes a size too small, where they are forced to conform and cannot move. Minds that are told they know all the answers are starved of questions. Minds that are trained to repeat only formulas make no discoveries of their own. It is possible for a mind to memorize every word of holy scripture and not know what it is saying. No, our minds were made to move, to change, to grow. We thrive on questions and live in difference. Not being sure is only an invitation, not a fault. The human mind is a beachcomber, not a paperweight. So here is another heresy: if the shoes are too tight, kick them off and run barefoot for a while.*

I have endless questions—questions that began long ago when I was a little boy and have stayed with me into my winter years, questions I will take with me wherever I go next. These questions prompted me to write this book. They are questions I shared in prayer and received an answer to when I stilled my mind and listened for the Spirit's response. These questions are the ladder I crafted deep within the kiva. These questions are bringing light into darkness.

DOUBTERS AND BELIEVERS. Doubt is the friend of faith. It exercises the strength of what we believe, pulling us forward with questions into new areas of spiritual exploration. To ask if anything is really out there, to wonder if there is a conscious creator, to insist on a reason for suffering: these are all the legitimate gifts of a doubting mind. We are doubters and believers, followers of a cycle of questions, testing our faith against our experiences. Faith is not an answer that never questions again any more than doubt is a question that never has anything but a single answer.

When we share our questions together, we become our own answer. We discover there is no one right way to do everything. We understand that no single plan will encompass the way forward. If we seek to bring light into darkness, then we must rely on the wisdom of us all. We listen to one another. We are patient with one another. We spend time with one another. Eventually, we trust one another because we see ourselves in one another. In other words, we go into the kiva together. We return to our place of beginning. We find our common ground. We share our stories.

PRAY WITH ME. Come sit with me, here beneath the shade, in the quiet corner of creation, and together we will sort out the worries of the world. We may not have the power to make things right with a single word, but we have words enough to speak the truth, and there is a power in truth greater than money can buy. From our bench we will survey the great garden of hope, growing in an abundance that knows no borders, welcoming the children of every land, sheltering the elders who stroll the paths of peace. Come pray with me, in any way you want, until our prayers appear like fireflies, here beneath the shade, telling us it is time to go, time to make our way home until another day.

I have made the climb I describe in these pages. I have reached the top of the ladder of my faith, and I have seen what waits for us there, if we will believe in it enough to try to reach it. I have looked into the four sacred directions. I have witnessed the moment when the earth and the sky meet in perfect balance. I have heard the voice of all my relatives from all the tribes of creation chanting the new morning into being. I have seen my ancestors gathering in the mist of first light, gathering with those of every nation under heaven. I am a witness, a scout of the sacred, come home to describe a hope that has no language to contain it. I wrote this book like a weaver, pulling together questions and answers, dreams and doubts, the messages of the Spirit and my own thoughts in prayer. Now I will sit beside you in the kiva, in the lodge, in the tent of our meeting. Now I will be silent so I can listen and learn, so I can discover if what I see is what you see, if our vision is truly the same.

SINCE TIME BEGAN. I have seen prayer flags fluttering in the thin and cold mountain air, bright bits of color against a turquoise sky, flags of love and compassion. I have seen candles flicker in the hushed vaults of cathedrals, tiny lights in the peaceful darkness, signs of longing and gratitude. I have seen dancers moving feathers and fringe beneath the moon, circling the drum that summons them, ancient steps retraced a thousand times. I have seen my own words rising, dreams of healing rising into stillness, streams of smoke rising from a fire burning since time began.

AFTERWORD

THE EMERGENCE

This book is a ladder. If you have climbed this far up with me, then you can already see what I see: the emergence.

The day has begun and the light is already over the horizon. The great change has started, and it will not stop until it is complete. It will not happen easily or quickly, but it will happen. What we now see only as darkness will be rolled back like a rug. The tribe of the human beings will climb the sacred ladder. We will climb together, all of us, with no exceptions. No one will be left behind.

We will climb into the light. We will come through the pains of birth, out into the daylight, and we will stand once more on the land we call our home. That land will be our mother and we will honor her for the life she has given us.

We will start again. We will rebuild what has been broken down. We will renew the kinship we have with our relatives. We will heal the scars of the past and begin to do what we were created to do: dance. We will dance in light. We will dance in hope. We will dance in truth.

This will happen. This is happening. The prophecy of this book is stronger than darkness because darkness is already a part of it. The kiva reminds us that we have been in darkness before. It is nothing new. Like an eclipse, it may shade the truth, but only for a while. Darkness can have no dominion over the tribe of the human beings. It can never be the last word, because darkness is always our beginning. We enter it only to be reborn again in the next cycle of our emergence. Through the kiva, we transform the darkness from threat to nurture. We take away its power. We channel it into the kiva—a place of worship, a place of faith and hope—and by so doing, we force the darkness to face the light. Once that happens, darkness disappears.

Do not be afraid. Do not be tricked into thinking what has been broken can never be fixed. Do not trade your freedom for an imagined safety in the shadows. Let this moment of darkness be the beginning of your next journey in faith.

Help others find the ladder. Share this book with as many people as you can. Show them the light you have discovered. Give it away. Let it grow.

Celebrate our diversity in the tribe of the human beings, for that is our strength and our future. Honor the earth. Respect the wisdom of the elders. Speak the truth. Do all of this, and you will be on the ladder to the light. And once you are there—once you have emerged into the world we are recreating—join the dance. Listen to the heartbeat of the drum, the endless cycles of dark and light, faith and fear, risk and renewal, and join the dance. Step out into the light and join the dance. The darkness will be no more. Beneath the bright, shining sun, join the dance and let the healing begin.

A WORLD OF LIGHT. *Sunrise is our banner, unfurled in a rising wind, the bright beacon of all our hopes, flying in the face of darkness, an old faith reborn, a new faith emerging, not for a few, but for all, the great tribes of life assembled, beneath the single blessing, a circle of light, light within light, healing the scars of shadows, releasing the soul of every captive, welcoming the stranger, honoring the elders, a world of light, spreading warmth to arms grown weary, lifting spirits to sing once more, uniting our family once again and forever, light flowing like a river, hope beating like a drum, up and out into the fields of harvest, unafraid and always thankful, the small light in a single heart that became the morning sun.*